ENEMIES *of* DESTINY

How David Prevailed

CONNIE HUNTER-URBAN

STUDY QUESTIONS INCLUDED

WESTBOW
PRESS®
A DIVISION OF THOMAS NELSON
& ZONDERVAN

WestBow Press books may be ordered through booksellers or by contacting:

WestBow Press
A Division of Thomas Nelson & Zondervan
1663 Liberty Drive
Bloomington, IN 47403
www.westbowpress.com
844-714-3454

ISBN: 978-1-6642-3799-5 (sc)
ISBN: 978-1-6642-3801-5 (hc)
ISBN: 978-1-6642-3800-8 (e)

Library of Congress Control Number: 2021912726

Print information available on the last page.

WestBow Press rev. date: 07/31/2021

CONTENTS

PART 3: DAVID'S FRIENDS, TURNED ENEMIES

ACKNOWLEDGEMENTS

I want to thank·

- My heavenly Father for downloading this assignment into me, sending me on this journey, helping me along the way, and being my rear guard.
- My husband, Wade, who stands beside me in every battle.
- My close friends who are constantly supportive— Margie, Curtis, Sharon.

FOREWORD

In the crucible of afflictions, trials, temptations, and persecution, a highly unlikely figure emerges from the sheepfolds of his father's flocks, as God's hand-picked chosen King. Who is this unknown lad who defies impossibilities? Who is this giant slayer armed merely with a primitive sling and a single stone? Who is this worshiping warrior? None other than David. None other than the only man ever described in sacred Scripture as having captured God's heart.

Connie Hunter-Urban unveils an intricate portrait of this multi-faceted shepherd-king. She uncovers the intrinsic nature and the hidden motives of David's heart, thus showing us how his gentleness made him great, how his determination to seek God's face granted him strategic victories. And most of all, we see an intensely passionate worshipper touching the heart of the Father so much, that Holy Spirit utterly consumes his sacrifices of praise, transforming David's rugged commonness into nothing short of royalty.

Delving into both David's private and public battles, Connie presents to us lessons we can learn from the vicious attacks by David's many enemies. Connie demonstrates to us how we can overcome every trap and snare set by the fowler of our soul. Enemies from without, nor enemies from within, can prevail against the submitted, well-trained warrior. A distinct anointing to equip and train you in the skillfully crafted weapons of our warfare comes forth through Connie's writing that grooms you for victory and breakthrough in even life's hardest challenges. Invaluable assets are also found in David's friends. Like running streams in the desert and flowers among thorns, David's true friends sustain him in his times of deepest drought and refresh him in the seasons of his deepest wounds. Saul's son Jonathan protects David when the insane king sought to kill him. Samuel, the prophet, brings divine inspiration, instruction, and guidance to David.

Nathan, the prophet, brings correction and chastisement to David, resulting in bitter tears of repentance. There is no man as destitute, as a man without friends; but at no time does the faithfulness of God allow David to be destitute of friends.

David heart responses throughout his life enlighten us to what God highly values: integrity, obedience, faithfulness, a forgiving heart, dependence upon the Holy Spirit, repentance, worship, and humility. When mad King Saul has a javelin in his hand, David responds with a worship in his hand. When God sends David men who were in distress, discontented, and in debt, he becomes a captain over them and grooms them into valiant men of war. When the prophet Nathan reprimands him for his sin, David mournfully and thoroughly repented. When Absalom attempts to usurp the throne, David searches his own heart. No matter the severity of the trial or circumstance, David's heart maintains a dedicated desire to please the God who called him, chose him, and anointed him. May our hearts do the same.

Dr. Cheryel K. Tarter, PhD, Theology, Covenant Bible College & Seminary
Co-Pastor, Bloodline of the King Ministries;
Apostle, The Launching Pad Revival Center, Hamilton, OH

PROLOGUE

DAVID'S REFLECTIONS

But my eyes are upon You, O GOD the Lord; in You I take
refuge; do not leave my soul destitute. Keep me from the
snares they have laid for me, and from the traps of the
workers of iniquity. Let the wicked fall into their own nets,
while I escape safely. (Ps. 141:8–10)

Purpose. Some search their whole lives to find it. However, as the Father's
unique workmanship, every Christian has a God-ordained purpose.
Whatever happens in our lives shapes us for how we accomplish our
purpose (see Eph. 2:10; 2 Pet. 1:5–7). I think of purpose like a staircase. We
climb one step at a time toward destiny; each level brings new experiences,
rewards, and challenges, so many factors influence our arriving at the goal.
We're taught and refined by steps our journey entails; then our feet claim
another plane.

Inching toward purpose is a process, but one thing is certain. As soon as
potential is revealed, satan attempts to derail the upward journey. He flings
whatever he can to force us to give up—family problems, health issues,
discouragement. Unfortunately, most people concede defeat. However, if
we really want that destiny God brought us to earth for, we must persevere
despite what's piled on each step to hinder ascension toward His plan. The
ultimate destination isn't the only priority of this expedition. Every phase
is important with its own purpose. When we arrive, we embark on new
journeys and must once again learn as we traverse new seasons. No matter
how difficult or numerous the steps, everything counts toward fulfilling
the promise of purpose.

DAVID

David's life shows these journeys aren't easy. When the stairway to his destiny was delineated, he didn't comprehend obstacles that awaited him. Like us, he filled various roles and had trials, successes, and failures. He was a victor; but sometimes, a victim. He had high highs and low lows. He sinned, yet repented. He was wise, but foolish. He cherished truth, but sometimes lied. He was loved, yet hated; supported, yet rejected; adored, yet persecuted. This mighty king was elevated, but humbled; confident, yet insecure. He kept his "heart...not haughty nor [his] eyes lofty" (see Ps. 131:1), despite accomplishments and others' exaltation of him. He knew how to repent and ask for God's grace while keeping persecutions in perspective. Though his destiny was a surety because he trusted God's promise, sometimes discouragement plagued him. Do these statements resemble your journey?

David's name, meaning "well-beloved, dear,"[1] depicts him with men and God. Saul's servants described him as "skillful in playing, a mighty man of valor, a man of war, prudent in speech, and a handsome person; and the Lord [was] with him" (1 Sam. 16:18). His men once said he was the "lamp of Israel" (2 Sam. 21:17). His lineage was even part of his destiny. After Jericho's fall, Rahab lived with the Hebrews and married Salmon. They had Boaz, whom Ruth married. She bore Obed, Jesse's dad. David was the youngest of Jesse's eight sons (see 1 Sam. 17:12). That lineage set up David's most important destiny achievement—being Jesus' forefather.

He's first mentioned when God told Samuel he was removing the kingdom from Saul and giving it to another. Historians believe Samuel anointed David for that purpose when he was about fifteen.[2] After his calling, he learned much by serving or eluding Saul, probably about ten years.[3] Surviving hardships and numerous enemies, he eventually reigned in Judah when he was thirty (see 2 Sam. 5:4). With seven and a half years there and thirty-three over all Israel, he reigned forty years (see 2 Sam. 5:4–5) and died at seventy, "full of days and riches and honor" (see 1 Chron. 29:27–28). As he shaped the great Israeli empire, his integrity and anointing set standards for future kings. He arrived at his God-ordained destiny, having endured much along the way.

ENEMIES

Like David, we should "Be sober, be vigilant; because your adversary the devil walks about like a roaring lion, seeking whom he may devour" (1 Pet. 5:8). He's constantly on the prowl, waiting to annihilate and derail our proceeding to a higher destiny level. He employs prolific weapons, but the most common is people. However, though one may be employed by satan to wield damaging weapons, we war against the devil, not those he uses as enemies (see Eph. 6:12). Jesus came to destroy satan's works (see 1 John 3:8), and He was surrounded by many the devil employed against Him. One of His select group betrayed Him; another denied Him. At times He traveled based on avoiding people who wanted to kill Him (see John 7:1) or called out those being manipulated by satan. He labeled Pharisees as a "brood of vipers," whose evil showed because one's mouth exemplifies his or her heart (see Matt. 12:34). God sees past misleading façades that blur a person's genuine character.

After the Lord told me to write my book, *Be Healed!*, my husband and I had two years of intense, varied enemy assaults. Many vicious and prolonged attacks were from people satan used as distractions to keep us from God's purpose. I had become discouraged in battle; then, I reread David's chapters. Holy Spirit led me to study and then write about how his enemies paralleled some attacking us and other Christians on their destiny journeys. I refer to them as David did—enemies. Many of his enemies were overt, while others hovered covertly. Some he loved most, later became enemies. His enemies show how satan uses others to keep us from moving into our purpose. I give *BEWARES* to spot signs that the devil's using someone as an enemy. Sometimes, though, our worst human enemies aren't others but ourselves, so we should assess our actions that could affect destiny. We choose our paths, and those choices serve us well or poorly as we bring each thought under control (see 2 Cor. 10:5).

Spiritual warfare is 24-7-365. Because of that, in addition to enemies, I also list David's weapons of warfare which worked with his God-directed, military prowess. This book's purpose is to explain that no matter who fights against us or what the agenda is, God's our answer. If He's our Everything, each battle will take us closer to destiny. David needed God often during his journey and called on Him regularly. His progress toward his destiny, victories, trust in God, and even doubts are recorded through frank reflections in his psalms. We can learn much by taking a journey with David.

Part One

DAVID'S ENEMIES

Chapter One

SAUL

DAVID'S REFLECTIONS

[When men watched David's house to kill him] Deliver
me from my enemies,...defend me from those who rise
up against me. Deliver me from workers of iniquity, and
save me from bloodthirsty men. For look, they lie in wait
for my life; the mighty gather against me.... They run
and prepare themselves through no fault of mine. (Ps.
59:1–4)

Enemies are everywhere; sometimes they are even kings who try to derail
our destinies. Saul's actions exemplify what *not* to do during your destiny
journey. He changed from loving to loathing David and demonstrated
how someone you respect can hurt you by protecting his position rather
than acquiescing to God's will. He represents leaders to whom we owe
submission even when they persecute to retain their status though they no
longer operate with the anointing. Saul began to reign when he was thirty
and ruled Israel forty-two years (see 1 Sam. 13:1 Christian Standard Bible).
David was his loyal subject, son-in-law, music therapist, worshipper, protégé,
captain, and son's best friend. He frequently showed love and mercy to the
king but received little in return. As God's choice for Israel's first king, "the
Lord...anointed [Saul as] commander over His inheritance" (1 Sam. 10:1).
His legacy should've been extraordinary, the one through whom the Lord's

kingdom would be established. However, that destiny stalled as his character affected his ability to reign. Thus, he forfeited his children's futures.

Beware: *Of those whose immaturity, character, and inexperience exceed their position.*

SAUL'S CALLING

During Samuel's years as judge, conflict hadn't existed between Israel and the Philistines after Samuel defeated them at Mizpah. Those dynamics likely would change because the Philistines knew Samuel was aged. When Israel wanted a king, Saul became God's first pick. He was "choice and... more handsome...than... [any of] the children of Israel" (1 Sam. 9:2), physically superior and a head taller than anyone. He's first mentioned when his father, Kish, a Benjamite and mighty man, lost his donkeys and sent Saul to Samuel to inquire about them. This problem was a nuisance that evolved into a divine encounter. Unbeknownst to Saul, God had told Samuel a Benjamite was coming. He should anoint that man as Israel's commander to save the nation from the Philistines (see 1 Sam. 7:12–13; 8:19; 9:3, 14–16). God had a plan for Saul, but he lost sight of how best to fulfill his destiny and didn't purge hindrances as he ran the race on which God had sent him (see Heb. 12:1).

Beware: *Of resenting bad situations rather than seeing God's hand in them.*

As we're tapped for our God-ordained assignments, humility is key. At first, Saul saw himself as a least-likely king candidate. Samuel anointed him and then said that the next day Saul would hear that the donkeys were recovered. He instructed Saul to go to Gilgal and wait until Samuel joined him to give offerings and instructions. When Samuel assembled Israel and called the tribe of Benjamin, Saul was missing. Hiding his tall frame behind equipment, he likely peeked around to see if this gathering was really about him or if he'd misunderstood. His meekness probably impressed Samuel, who later changed his mind as Saul's true character emerged. His actions showed either humility or reluctance to be king, but both traits later changed. When pride settles in, destiny is affected. Most acknowledged

Saul's anointing as king, but certain rebels wondered how Saul could save them. They showed lack of respect and support for the potential king, so they brought him no presents. This represented a great slight, but Saul said or did nothing against them (see 1 Sam. 9:21; 10:1–2, 8, 17–22, 27). Later, insults mattered much. Though others may not respect our calling, we must allow God to fight for our destinies.

Beware: *Of those whose humility is replaced by pride after their promotion.*

Saul stepped into destiny as he won people's hearts by his actions in his first battle as leader. The Ammonite king made an atrocious proposal—Israelites must put out their own right eyes. When Saul returned from tending herds and heard this ultimatum, Holy Spirit came upon him. Angrily, he cut up oxen and sent them to all Israel as a call to action. He divided responders into three groups; they killed Ammonites until noon. Then the rest "scattered, so that no two of them were left together" (1 Sam. 11:11). As a result, people supported Saul and wanted to kill those who'd questioned his reign. He refused because God had saved Israel. Samuel then called people to Gilgal so he could set up the kingdom and officially make Saul king. Despite great rejoicing, Samuel reminded them that a king wasn't God's will, but they persisted (see 1 Sam. 11:1–7, 12–15; 12:1–2, 12). Established as king, Saul waged war against the Philistines and other enemies (see 1 Sam. 14:47–48). Wherever he went, he "vexed his enemies" (1 Sam. 14:47 KJV).

Beware: *Of giving in to enemy demands.*

GOD'S REJECTION

Promotion is our journey's goal; once we achieve God's purpose, growth and obedience shouldn't stop. Twice, Saul's actions proved his character and offended God. First, he disobeyed Samuel's orders and sacrificed without the prophet. Then, he didn't destroy all Amalekites. As a result, Samuel said God had rejected him as king. God has a purpose for His edicts and doesn't change His mind after we're promoted. In fact, "the counsel of the LORD stands forever, the plans of His heart to all generations" (see Ps.

33:11). Fulfilling those plans depends upon our choices, and disobedience is a mitigating factor. Saul admitted his guilt of fearing and obeying people rather than God and asked for forgiveness and to accompany Samuel to worship. Samuel refused and reiterated God's rejection. When Saul grabbed the prophet's robe and ripped it, Samuel spoke a prophetic analogy that God would tear Saul's kingdom from him (see 1 Sam. 13:12; 15:9–11, 24–28). Saul forfeited his bright destiny and legacy for his sons.

Beware: *Of brethren or leadership from whom God removes His anointing.*

Saul's loss prepared David's destiny path. When David began helping him, Saul "loved him greatly" and made David his armor bearer (1 Sam. 16:21). On their way home from Goliath's defeat, Israel's army was probably ecstatic, high-fiving and dancing down the road. A win over the giant would bring David much favor because of Saul's promises for defeating Goliath. His future seemed glorious—living full time with his beloved king, having a new-found soulmate in Jonathan, marrying into their family, and helping his dad financially. However, David's victories and promotions were the beginning of blessings and persecutions. Saul was plagued by evil spirits, so his integrity plummeted. Many open doors allowed his devolving character—pride, jealousy, disobedience. One huge door for enemy access is fear. Saul was afraid of many things regarding David—he'd take the kingdom, the Lord was with him, David behaved wisely, his daughter loved him (see 1 Sam. 18:12, 15, 28–29). However, the greatest open door for demonic presence was that, "the Spirit of the Lord [had] departed from Saul, [so] a distressing spirit…troubled him" (1 Sam. 16:14). When Holy Spirit leaves, a void exists for the devil to enter. As their relationship grew flawed and doomed, David moved closer to his destiny while Saul's eroded.

Beware: *Of those influenced by evil spirits.*

SAUL'S JEALOUSY

Saul's negativity toward David began "when David was returning from the slaughter of the Philistine" (see 1 Sam. 18:6). This probably wasn't referring to Goliath but to Philistine battles where Saul sent David after he'd killed the giant.[1] As the warriors returned, they celebrated. Women were singing and dancing with tambourines, and musicians were meeting the army. Saul was pleased, probably waving and smiling at their adoration. Then he heard their chants: "Saul has slain his thousands, and David his ten thousands" (1 Sam. 18:7). His smile faded into disbelief then anger as these lavish praises of David elevated the servant above the master. Jealousy's a cancer that damages Christians and cancels their assignments. Moses called it an evil spirit. It's also listed as flesh works along with adultery, idolatry, and sorcery. Paul says we won't inherit God's kingdom if we practice these things (see Num. 5:14; Gal. 5:19 21). David witnessed its results with Saul, so he realized a person could become infected and was careful in later encounters. Certain behaviors prevent promotions.

Beware: *Of feeling envious about others' promotions.*

All believers have a place in God's plan. His using another isn't to be envied but celebrated. We're part of His army and working for the same goal—victory over the enemy as we fulfill godly purpose. Each army position is crucial, and no one's is exactly like another's. Paul explains this when he compares the church body working together to the physical body's operation. We're members of the same body (see Rom. 12:5), which doesn't function as well without its other parts. Daniel demonstrated caring about others' roles in the body. After he and his intercessors prayed about the king's dream and received revelation and interpretation, he was promoted. However, he also recommended advancement for friends who'd been part of the prayer team (see Dan. 2:17–18, 48–49). When we promote self or look with envy at another's assignment and victories, we make the Christian body operate ineffectively. Those feelings change us and our relationship with the Lord and others. That, in turn, affects destiny.

Beware: *Of those who don't value all parts of the Christian body.*

After praise of David, Saul didn't acknowledge him as a force for Israel or celebrate his ending the Goliath threat. Instead, he perceived him as a threat to his kingship. Hatred consumed him, so he wondered, "what more can [David] have but the kingdom?" (1 Sam. 18:8). After the victory over

Goliath, Saul had brought him to live with him and not return to Jesse's house. Eventually, though, he removed David from his presence and made him captain over 1,000 men of war. Saul probably thought of this as a reduction in rank; instead, David was accepted and loved by Israel and Judah (see 1 Sam. 18:2, 13–16). This became a valuable tool by affording him an opportunity to learn, excel, and grow in favor among others as "he went out and came in before [Israel]" (1 Sam. 18:16). Sometimes what looks like demotion is actually another step toward promotion.

Beware: *Of actions of those with self-serving motives.*

RAMPING UP HATE

Favor and promise of promotion will be intensely fought by the enemy. Because Saul knew of David's popularity and calling as king, he connived for David's demise. When he promised David his older daughter, Merab, David humbly asked, "what is my life or my father's family in Israel, that I should be son-in-law to the king?" (see 1 Sam. 18:18). He didn't seem to remember that Saul had already pledged her to anyone who killed Goliath. Saul's second vow of marriage to Merab became his second broken promise. When David should've married Merab, Saul gave her to Adriel instead. Then, when the king was told his other daughter, Michal, loved David, he offered her as David's wife. The dowry would be 100 Philistine foreskins. Saul's first promises hadn't been honored, and now this offer was a ploy. As he'd contemplated and voiced previously, Saul wanted the Philistines to kill David; technically, he wouldn't have committed the murder. His tactics didn't work. After David and his men killed 200 Philistines and brought their foreskins to Saul, David received Michal in marriage (see 1 Sam. 17:25; 18:17–20, 25–27).

Beware: *Of believing one who previously reneged on promises.*

After he'd learned of Michal's love for David, Saul was reminded that God was with David. He became even more afraid of him and was "David's enemy continually" (1 Sam. 18:29). In other words, David remained Saul's adversary for life. Wherever he was sent, David "behaved wisely" (see 1 Sam.

18:14). As Saul grew more suspicious and determined to eliminate him, David traveled with the army, behaved more wisely than Saul's servants, and was highly esteemed. Saul's behavior, however, grew more unwise. Though his actions turned increasingly evil, erratic, and vindictive, David knew that even God's wayward anointed are off limits (see 1 Sam. 18:29–30; 24:6). He remained loyal because he knew others' evil actions could be overcome with his good (see Rom. 12:21). This lesson serves us well as we prepare to step into destiny.

Beware: *Of leaders with unwise behavior.*

MURDEROUS SAUL

Jealousy brings much evil, and Saul's character eroded so drastically that he planned and attempted David's murder. He told Jonathan and his servants to kill David, but Jonathan loved his friend and wouldn't harm him. Saul tried to kill him twice while David was playing music to calm demons. An adversary often attacks while we're helping others, operating under the anointing, or threatening to cast him from another person. Once, while David played to calm the distressing spirit, Saul sat, spear in hand. He attempted to trap David against the wall; but David slipped away. Instead, Saul drove the spear into the wall. Another time after David struck a mighty blow against the Philistines, Saul, under demonic influence, tried to pin David against the wall with a spear. David again escaped (see 1 Sam. 19:1; 18:10–11; 19:9–10). When a person tries to resurrect an anointing, integrity plummets.

Beware: *Of those who ask you to perform ungodly acts.*

David's marriage to Michal was another of Saul's plans for David's destruction. Saul sent messengers to watch David's house and kill him in the morning, but Michal warned David and let him down from a window. She laid an image (idol in NIV) with clothes and goats' hair in the bed and told Saul's messengers David was sick. When they tried to capture him, they discovered the image instead. Saul confronted Michal about her deception; she said David threatened to kill her if she didn't help (see 1 Sam.

19:11–17). Lying to her dad by maligning David's character to save herself showed her fear of Saul's retribution. After this, David could no longer live around him. He memorialized this murder attempt by writing that "at evening they return, they growl like a dog" (Ps. 59:14). At this time, David probably wondered if God remembered his calling. However, everything we suffer accomplishes something in us.

SAUL'S DEPRAVITY

Choices touch others, ourselves, and destiny. David fled from Saul and went to Nob to seek help from priests. This incident showed flaws in David, especially because no mention was made of his seeking God's will. God gives wisdom liberally, but we need to ask (see James 1:5). David sought refuge with Ahimelech, high priest and Eli's great-grandson (see 1 Sam. 14:3; 22:9). Ahimelech had been in charge of the tabernacle at Shiloh, but it was moved to Nob after Philistines captured the ark. Later, it would be transferred to Gibeon.[2] David came to Nob alone, so Ahimelech knew something was wrong. When David professed to be on secret business for Saul and had left his men elsewhere, his lie endangered these priests. Truth may have changed a horrendous outcome. Ahimelech believed him, so David asked for five loaves of bread or whatever Ahimelech had. Only holy bread was available and just for those celibate for a time period. David assured him the men hadn't been with women for three days. Though Ahimelech violated God's law that reserved this bread for priests, often necessity supersedes law. Jesus referred to this when He, too, disregarded an established law by plucking grain and eating on the Sabbath (see 1 Sam. 21:1–5; Matt. 12:3–4).

Beware: *Of consequences of lies, even though they seem necessary.*

David's lie made Ahimelech an unknowing participant against the king when Abimelech gave David provisions. David then asked for a spear or sword. Only Goliath's sword was there, so David took it. That detail is interesting. Unlike his prior encounter with the giant, David now thought he needed a traditional weapon. He'd likely become exhausted by Saul's persistent pursuits and had fallen into fear's camp. While at Nob, David saw Doeg, Saul's chief herdsmen, skulking about (see 1 Sam. 21:6–9). As Esau's descendant, he wasn't an Israelite. However, for an unknown reason he was "detained before the Lord" (1 Sam. 21:7). This could've been because of a vow, uncleanness, or crime.[3] Nob priests paid dearly for both David's and Doeg's presences.

Beware: *Of the enemy of fear that creeps into God's generals and ends in devastating results.*

Saul tried to locate David. With rising suspicion, he felt servants had conspired against him. He asked if David had promised promotions or land to follow him and said they should've informed him about David and Jonathan's covenant. Doeg revealed that he'd seen David at Nob, where priests had helped him. Saul called for Ahimelech and the priests and asked why they'd conspired against him. Ahimelech said he inquired of God for David but didn't know problems existed between Saul and David. He spoke of David's faithfulness, obedience, and honor to the king. Saul probably interpreted that defense of David as proof of treason. Obviously, he'd become depraved enough to believe priests were expendable. He commanded servants to kill Ahimelech and his sons (all priests), but servants wouldn't comply (see 1 Sam. 22:7–17).

Beware: *Of those whose paranoia causes them to suspect even God's faithful.*

Stepping into destiny can't be by sacrificing others. At Saul's orders, Doeg killed the priests. He may have wanted to advance himself by pleasing Saul, but that ambition was at a great cost. He massacred eighty-five priests, plus women, children, and infants in Nob. One of Ahimelech's priests, Abiathar, escaped and went to David. Eventually, he'd serve David throughout his reign. When he told David about Saul's actions, David grieved because he should've protected them after he saw Doeg at Nob and knew his potential for wickedness (see 1 Sam. 22:18–22). David later wrote about how Doeg "boast[ed] in evil" (Ps. 52:1) by telling Saul about David. When Holy Spirit whispers in our ear, we should pay attention.

Beware: *Of ignoring Holy Spirit's warnings.*

THE PURSUIT

Sometimes those we think will protect us, don't. Saul was told that David was at Keilah. He claimed God delivered David to him because he was trapped by Keilah's gates and bars. He called for war against David. David asked God if he'd be turned over to Saul. The Lord confirmed that Keilah's men would betray him though David had just saved them from Philistines. They'd likely heard of Saul's wrath at Nob and now feared retribution if they helped David. David and his men left Keilah, so Saul stopped pursuing. Then Ziphites told Saul where David was hiding (see 1 Sam. 23:7–13, 19). Saul and his men followed, but David was alerted. David wrote that "strangers" (the Ziphites) had come against him, and the "oppressor" (Saul) sought his life (Ps. 54:3). Saul heard David had fled, so he followed to the Wilderness of Maon. His and David's armies were positioned on opposite sides of the mountain, so David couldn't escape. God intervened. A messenger told Saul that Philistines had invaded Israel, so he quit pursuing David to go to war with the Philistines. This place became known as the Rock of Escape (see 1 Sam. 23:25–28). God can use even enemy actions to protect our callings.

Beware: *Of those who may turn on you to protect themselves.*

God safeguards callings, but sometimes our journey takes us to strange places. David left the wilderness and settled in the En Gedi strongholds. Saul returned from encounters with Philistines and took 3,000 choice men to seek David. Although En Gedi housed many caves, Saul went into one to use the bathroom. David and his men were hiding in the back of that particular cave, at that particular time. His men said God had delivered Saul, so David should kill him (see 1 Sam. 23:29; 24:1–4). These were Saul's words about David at Keilah, but now they were true. God makes seemingly random encounters be part of His plan! This intersection was God's hand, but not so David could destroy Saul. This created an opportunity for David to behave wisely again. One purpose of battles is to refine our mettle that will serve us well for destiny.

Beware: *Of thinking God put enemies into your hand for their destruction.*

Because of this event, the two men's characters were again contrasted. Though Saul pursued to destroy God's anointed, David restrained his men from killing God's formerly anointed. Instead, he secretively crept behind Saul and cut off a piece of his robe. Later, he was bothered for doing that because the robe was a symbol of Saul's kinghood. David had no right to harm it but should, "honor all people. Love the brotherhood. Fear God. Honor the king" (1 Pet. 2:17). At Saul's death, his armor bearer also understood that concept and showed deference. When Saul asked the servant to kill him, he refused because he was afraid of God's vengeance on whoever harmed God's anointed (see 1 Sam. 24:4–6; 1 Chron. 10:4).

Beware: *Of lifting your hand against leadership.*

After Saul left the cave, David went outside and shouted to ask why Saul believed people claiming David wanted to harm him. He told Saul he could've killed him and was advised to do so. He showed the swatch of the robe as proof he didn't have rebellion or evil toward him. Saul wept as he recognized the voice because David had returned good to him instead of the evil he'd given David. He'd dealt righteously with the king though God delivered him to David. Saul acknowledged David's anointing and asked him to swear he wouldn't cut off his descendants. David complied, and Saul went home. Their relationship seemed healed, but David knew the difference between remorse and repentance. He and his men hid in their stronghold, and Saul didn't abandon persecuting or hurting David. He gave Michal to another man (see 1 Sam. 24:7–11, 16–22; 25:44). Hurtful deeds our enemies do will someday work for our good.

Beware: *Of those whose past shows their remorse will be short-lived.*

ANOTHER ACT OF LOVE

Part of God's work in us during our journey is to teach us to love, even enemies. When Saul heard where David was hiding, he again took 3,000 men to find him. Spies told David Saul's location, so they sneaked into Saul's camp while they slept. The king had a spear in the ground by his head. Abishai said God had once again delivered Saul into David's hand, and they should slay Saul with his own spear. How ironic! That spear was probably the one Saul had clutched numerous times to fling at his rival. David could've finished this problem, but he wasn't thinking of payback. Having just seen foolish Nabal's fate, David knew God would avenge. He said Saul was still God's anointed. The Lord would judge and strike Saul down, or he'd perish in battle. He grabbed the spear and jug of water from beside Saul's head, and they crept away in darkness. No one knew they'd been there because God made them sleep deeply (see 1 Sam. 26:1–12). God will orchestrate circumstances, and sometimes His weapon to protect our callings is as simple as sleep.

Beware: *Of your character that seeks revenge.*

David went to a far-off hill and shouted for the army to see what he'd taken from above the king's head. When Saul again recognized the voice, he called David his son. David asked why he pursued him when he'd done no evil toward the king. He said if the Lord stirred Saul up against him, he'd sacrifice to God to repent. However, if men made statements that caused Saul to pursue, he spoke curses on them. Saul vowed not to harm David because he'd again spared his life. He called himself a fool who'd "erred exceedingly" (1 Sam. 26:21). David told Saul to send someone to retrieve the spear. Then he said God would recompense David's righteousness for sparing him. He asked God to value David's life like he'd valued Saul's and deliver him from tribulation. Saul pronounced a blessing that David would do great things and ultimately prevail (see 1 Sam. 26:13–14, 17–25). Even persecutors know when God's favor and calling rest on us.

Beware: *Of becoming discouraged by others' unfair acts.*

WITCH OF EN DOR

No matter where we are on this destiny journey, God's laws remain. Saul lost his kingdom due to disobedience. Now, he again disobeyed God's law and his own orders against dealing with the occult, particularly calling back the dead (see Deut. 18:11). After Samuel died, Saul put mediums and spiritists out of Israel. As honorable as Saul's decree was, he now committed an atrocity. When Philistines amassed a large army, "his heart trembled greatly" (1 Sam. 28:5). He sought to hear from God, who didn't speak through a dream, the Urim, or a prophet. While Samuel was alive, Saul hadn't sought relationship with God but rather with Samuel. Now, God had become his enemy, Saul's "stone of stumbling" (Isa. 8:14). His silence prompted Saul to commit a forbidden act (see 1 Sam. 28:3–6).

Beware: *Of hopelessness that causes you to do ungodly things.*

Being desperate to hear from the Lord regarding the upcoming battle, Saul sent his servant for a medium. They found one at En Dor. He disguised himself, took two men, and approached at night. Obviously, he knew this was wrong because he used camouflage and cover of darkness to avoid recognition. He probably glanced around furtively and jumped at each sound because of his ungodly mission, yet he persisted. When he asked for a séance, the witch accused him of attempting to snare her because of Saul's edict. The act was more deplorable when Saul swore by God she wouldn't get in trouble. When he asked her to resurrect Samuel, she realized his identity and asked why he'd deceived her. He said not to be afraid and asked what she saw. She described the spirit of an old man covered with a mantle and then cried out loudly in fear. When Saul recognized Samuel, he bowed. While Samuel was alive, Saul had ignored his directions. Now, he was desperate enough to talk with the dead prophet. When Samuel asked why Saul had summoned him, Saul said to receive instructions about the Philistines because God wasn't speaking to him anymore. Samuel said God had departed and was now Saul's enemy. Because of disobedience He'd torn the kingdom from Saul's hand and given it to David. He prophesied that the next day Philistines would defeat Israel, and Saul and his sons would die (see 1 Sam. 28:7–19).

Beware: *Of those who stand for righteousness until it's inconvenient.*

Afraid because of Samuel's words, Saul fell to the ground. He hadn't eaten in a day and a night, so the medium offered bread. At first he refused; then others urged him to eat, so he relented. She prepared food for Saul and his men, who ate and then left (see 1 Sam. 28:20, 22–25). Though Saul should've repented and called out to God, he ate. Ironically, at one of his first battles, he'd ordered his men not to eat; now at the end, he ate. When "there was no strength in [Saul]" (1 Sam. 28:20), he found his power in food. In contrast, when David and his men were distraught, "David strengthened himself in the Lord" (see 1 Sam. 30:4, 6). The next day, Saul and his sons were killed as Samuel had prophesied. Unfortunately, Saul died because he was unfaithful to the Lord, didn't obey His word, and consulted a medium instead of God (see 1 Chron. 10:13–14). This ignoble death contrasts with David's, who simply "rested with his fathers" (1 Kings 2:10). Saul and his family paid a great price for forfeiture of his calling.

AFTER SAUL'S DEATH

Even after an enemy's death, we shouldn't rejoice. Three days after Saul and his sons' deaths, word reached David in Ziklag. An Amalekite came from Saul's camp and told David he'd finished Saul's unsuccessful suicide attempt. Although this could have occurred, the prior account of Saul's death doesn't tell this story. More likely, the Amalekite was lying to impress David. In warfare, enemy lies have enough truth to convince others and gain favor with leadership. However, David didn't react with gratitude or joy at Saul's destruction. When the man displayed the king's crown and bracelet, David grieved all day. Then, he ordered the Amalekite's death because he'd killed God's anointed (see 2 Sam. 1:1–15).

Beware: *Of enemy lies presented as truth.*

The Philistines exacted retribution for David's defeat of their champion. They put Saul's armor in their god's temple like the Hebrews had put Goliath's sword in theirs. They fastened his body to the wall and placed Saul's head in Dagon's temple like David had taken Goliath's to Jerusalem. To keep Saul's and his sons' bodies from being further mutilated or humiliated, the men of Jabesh Gilead stole their bodies from where the Philistines had hanged them (see 1 Chron. 10:9–12). Those men burned them at Jabesh, buried their bones under the tamarisk tree, and fasted seven days. When David was told what they did for Saul and his sons, he spoke blessings over them and said he'd repay with kindness (see 1 Sam. 31:11–13; 2 Sam. 2:4–7). This act likely showed Israel that David wouldn't pursue those loyal to Saul.

Later, famine prevailed for three years. When David asked God the cause, He said Saul and his men had killed Gibeonites. This was a sin because that nation had covenant with Israel through Joshua. Although they weren't part of Israel and covenant was made through deception, Israel had vowed protection. God expected Israel to continue honoring that covenant (see Josh. 9:15). David asked the Gibeonites how he could rectify Saul's mistake. They didn't want money from his family or the death of anyone in Israel but for seven of Saul's descendants to be hanged. David responded to their requests but spared Mephibosheth because of his and Jonathan's oath. If David had offered Mephibosheth, he'd have honored one covenant while violating another. Instead, he gave Saul's other descendants, including five of Merab's sons with Adriel and two of Saul's sons with Rizpah, his concubine (see 2 Sam. 21:1 8).

Beware: *Of ungodly actions that follow you, even in death.*

Rizpah had been mentioned when Ishbosheth accused Abner of being with her after Saul's death (see 2 Sam. 3:7). Her sons and the others were hanged in the first days of barley harvest. Rizpah mourned her sons by spreading sackcloth so she could lie on a rock and protect their bodies from birds and beasts. She guarded them "from the beginning of harvest until the late rains poured on them" (2 Sam. 21:10). From planting season to late rains, Rizpah could have remained with her sons' bodies as long as six months.[4] After King David heard about her devotion, he reverenced her sons. He took Saul's and Jonathan's bones from Jabesh and buried theirs and the hanged men's bones in Saul's father's tomb. Because of honoring Saul's covenant, famine ended (see 2 Sam. 21:9–14). That scenario speaks to me. We should prayerfully stand guard over our children. Their situations may be stinking, but we need to avert the enemy's plunder. The King will honor that.

CONCLUSION

Enemies to destiny arise, even as beloved leadership. David wrote that God "delivered me from my strong enemy, from those who hated me, for they were too strong for me. They confronted me in the day of my calamity, but the LORD was my support... [and] delivered me because He delighted in me" (Ps.18:17–19). David was on his destiny path, surrounded by many who wanted to prevent that. But the Lord was stronger than David's strongest haters. He supported and delighted in David. He'll do the same for us as we journey to make His will become our reality.

DAVID'S WEAPONS: OBEDIENCE

DAVID'S REFLECTIONS

> The fear of the LORD is clean, enduring forever; the
> judgments of the LORD are true and righteous altogether.
> More to be desired are they than gold…; sweeter also than
> honey and the honeycomb. Moreover by them Your servant
> is warned, and in keeping them there is great reward. (Ps.
> 19:9–11)

As David traveled his destiny road, he refined an amazing weapon of
warfare—obedience. Even though we don't understand why God wants us
to do something His way, whatever He asks, our answer should be, "Yes!"
His ways are perfect (see Ps. 18:30), and obedience is a sign of our love for
Him: "If you love [Him], [you'll] keep [His] commandments" (John 14:15).
Obedience demonstrates respect for the Father while disobedience shows
the opposite. Submission is a trait we must learn before going into destiny,
and complying with those in authority teaches how to obey our Father (see
Heb. 13:17). We should defer to many: pastors, parents, spouses, bosses,
policemen, and "governing authorities" (Rom. 13:1), even those like Saul
who treat us unfairly. Some people have wonderful potential that can never
be realized because they never learn the submission lesson. If we can't
submit to earthly authorities, how can we to God?

Obedience doesn't just happen one day but is refined by a lifetime of
practicing submission. Our compliance to the Lord shouldn't be grudging,
but unquestioning and immediate. When God told Abraham to sacrifice
his beloved son, the next morning he rose early, saddled the donkey, split
wood, and departed to where God told him (see Gen. 22:3). When the angel
told the young Mary she would conceive, she said, "Let it be to me according
to your word" (Luke 1:38). After Philip was involved with a great Samaritan
revival where multitudes received miracles, God told him to leave that
revival and minister to only one person (see Acts 8:5–7, 29). He responded
like we should: "Philip ran to him" (Acts 8:30). Willing obedience brings
God's blessings and allows us to partake of the land's spoils rather than be

defeated. It makes our adversaries be God's foes, too (see Isa. 1:19; Exod. 23:22).

David learned to obey as a boy. Although everyone was probably excited about the prophet's visit, his brothers were in the house with Samuel while David watched sheep. When his dad told him to take supplies to his brothers, the next morning, "David rose early" to obey (1 Sam. 17:20). When Saul gave orders, he respected and obeyed, even when the king had ulterior motives. Part of David's last recorded words were about "ruling in the fear of God" and "sons of rebellion" (2 Sam. 23:3, 6). Paul later referred to "sons of disobedience," who act according to satan (Eph. 2:2). For Saul, disobedience opened the door to satanic attack and forfeiture of his destiny. Obedience took David into his destiny. It's our journey's foundation, too.

Beware: *Of those who disobey authority figures.*

SAUL'S DISOBEDIENCE

Saul made choices like the world does—they want what *they* want rather than God's will. While awaiting a battle with the Philistines, he disobeyed the Lord. He'd waited for Samuel seven days as the prophet had instructed. When troops grew afraid of the upcoming skirmish, they scattered, and Saul panicked. Against God's law and Samuel's instructions, he performed a burnt offering. When Samuel arrived, Saul didn't accept responsibility for his actions. He blamed his decisions on others—the people for leaving and Samuel for coming late. He scolded Saul and spoke God's judgment against him: He'd lose the kingdom for his family (see 1 Sam. 13:5–14).

Beware: *Of leaders who blame others for their poor decisions.*

Saul's destiny and legacy as Israel's first king was derailed because of disobedience. Despite those drastic consequences, he again disobeyed when he later didn't kill the Amalekite king, Agag. He also kept the best livestock. The night before, God had told Samuel He regretted choosing Saul as king because of disobedience. Samuel grieved and "cried out to the Lord all night" (1 Sam. 15:11). This use of "cried out" means a "wild scream or shriek of supplication."[1] He loved Saul, cried uncontrollably for his loss, and interceded for him. However, when he traveled to meet the king, he witnessed personally Saul's devolving character. People said Saul had gone to Carmel, erected himself a monument, and then proceeded to Gilgal. Ironically, Gilgal was where before he was anointed king, he'd patiently awaited Samuel's instructions (see 1 Sam. 15:8–9, 12; 10:8). How Saul had changed from hiding prior to his coronation to building a personal monument! After we step into destiny, rules of obedience don't change.

Beware: *Of self-promoting leaders.*

As Samuel approached, Saul added lies to disobedience. He claimed he'd performed God's command for destruction. Unfortunately, he was more concerned with Samuel's approval than with God's. When Samuel heard animal noises, Saul made excuses and again blamed others for what should've been destroyed. Samuel told him to be quiet. He said the Lord had anointed him king though he was small, even in his own eyes. God sent him on a mission and told him how to perform it, but he hadn't obeyed and thus done evil. Saul again rationalized about why his actions were justified—to sacrifice the best to God. Samuel nor God bought that explanation. To obey the Lord, Samuel hacked Agag into pieces (see 1 Sam. 15:13–21, 33). Perhaps he did this to circumvent future problems with Agag or avoid God's wrath on the entire nation for disobedience.

Beware: *Of those who flagrantly disobey God and feel justified.*

TO OBEY

Like Saul rationalized, we put a good spin on disobedience when we logically reason why what we do is okay, even admirable. However, if we disregard God's word, we're wrong, and that affects destiny. No matter how we justify actions, that's disobedience. Several years ago, I felt led to pray and fast on Mondays, but the Lord gave me an additional order—don't fast when I traveled. I had stayed overnight in Michigan for a Monday morning book interview. When I woke up that morning at my hotel, I felt fine, so I fasted.

By the time I was supposed to leave for the studio, I was so weak I could barely hold up my head. Fasting or sacrificing to God is good, but we should differentiate between good things and God things. It's about obedience, even though we're doing something we think will please Him. Through Samuel, God told Saul that "to obey is better than sacrifice" (1 Sam. 15:22). Even if His ways aren't ours, we should obey. After Saul's disobedience, God anointed another in his place because God "removes kings and raises up kings" (Dan. 2:21). He doesn't change his mind, but sometimes our freewill and disobedience obstruct destiny.

Beware: *Of those in leadership who forget God's ways are above their own.*

I once heard a speaker say suffering is a teacher. I love the personification of that word. It's a picture of suffering, poised at the blackboard to direct our actions. Suffering imparts much, and one hard-learned lesson is obedience. Even with our Lord, "though He was a Son, yet He learned obedience by the things which He suffered" (Heb. 5:8). Wow! Jesus had to learn obedience, just as we do, and suffering made that happen! Those obedience lessons led Him to the greatest test of submission—the cross. Suffering is for a season to teach us obedience and other things, so we can receive the promised destiny (see Heb. 10:36). Do you remember what suffering produced in you?

CONTRASTS

Many examples show contrasts between the two kings' obedience. David, who consummately loved God, sometimes operated in disobedience. Unlike Saul, though, he accepted responsibility and repented for his decisions and moral failures. Twice, Saul admitted guilt, saying "I have sinned [against] the commandment of the Lord" (1 Sam. 15:24, 30). David later used nearly these same words but the difference speaks to me—"I have sinned against the Lord" (2 Sam. 12:13). The distinction about sinning against God's laws or against God shows the kings' hearts. Saul knew God only as a lawgiver. David had relationship with the Giver. He displayed repentance for his sins while Saul exhibited remorse and sorrow about his sin's consequences. David received forgiveness while Saul didn't. Later, Saul showed his heart as he sought the dead prophet through a medium while David approached God through a prophet.

Beware: *Of leaders who don't have relationship with the Father.*

Despite his understanding God's command and knowing Saul's fate, his sin with Bathsheba wasn't David's only example of disobedience. Once, he ordered Joab to number Judah and Israel. Afterwards, he felt condemned. Maybe God was displeased with the numbering because David hadn't sought His will, or perhaps David's actions implied Israel was strong by its large numbers. Chronicles says "satan...moved David to number Israel" (1 Chron. 21:1). Samuel says, "the Lord...moved David to...number Israel and Judah" (2 Sam. 24:1). This is a seeming contradiction; but since we can't be tempted by God (see James 1:13), sometimes He *allows* satan to influence choices. However, God can use our mistakes to bring about something great. Because of the numbering, David located the future site for God's temple (see 2 Chron. 3:1).

CONCLUSION

In battle, we're responsible to obey orders. God wants to work on our behalf, but He can't if we operate in disobedience. Though David knew to obey, he also knew to repent. David loved God and said, "I delight to do Your will, O my God" (Ps. 40:8). His experiences taught him much about delighting in doing God's will and obeying even in small things. Those lessons honed his weapons for assignments God would give—shepherd, warrior, king. Obeying God shows our love and is a great tool to propel us toward destiny.

QUESTIONS TO PONDER
(Answers in Appendix)
SAUL

1. How did Saul's character change after he was king?

2a. What chant did Saul hear people say about David?

2b. What emotions arose in him?

3. Give examples of when Saul tried to kill David.

4. What happened at Nob?

5. Give two times David spared Saul's life.

6a. Why did Saul go to a medium?

6b. What was his punishment?

OBEDIENCE

7a. With what attitude should we obey?

7b. Give biblical examples of those who obeyed this way.

8a. Why did God become angry with Saul after he fought the Amalekites?

8b. What character traits did his actions demonstrate?

9. What does "to obey is better than sacrifice" mean?

10. How did David disobey by numbering?

Something to Consider: How does David's enemy/weapon in these chapters speak about our enemies/weapons today?

Chapter Two

ABSALOM

DAVID'S REFLECTIONS

But You, O LORD, are a shield for me, my glory and the
One who lifts up my head. I cried to the LORD with my
voice, and He heard me from His holy hill. (Ps. 3:3–4)

Some enemies are those we love but who surreptitiously plot against
fulfillment of our destinies. Some of David's sons fall into that category.
He loved them and didn't question their motives although he should've.
They were spoiled, strong-willed, duplicitous, and hurtful. Absalom was the
most notable. Ironically, his name means "father of peace"; [1] but he caused
much hurt and turmoil to his father, family, and nation. More than once, he
belied his name by creating strife and sorrow. Of royal heritage from both
parents, Absalom was David's third son from his wife Maacah, daughter of
Talmai, king of Geshur (see 2 Sam. 3:3). With royal lineage on both sides,
Absalom's destiny could have been mighty, but undesirable character traits
disqualified him.

Beware: *Of those you love dearly but who can hurt you most.*

The first reference to him was when David's children were born in
Hebron. After that, when David was king of Israel, Tamar's story was told.
Three sons and a daughter (Tamar) were born to Absalom (see 2 Sam.

13:1; 14:27). His daughter being named after his sister shows his love for her. Absalom's sons weren't identified and must've died young because at his death he had no sons. He was handsome and praised more than anyone else for his good looks. Each year when he cut his hair, it weighed 200 shekels, about five pounds.[2] Hebrews regarded their leaders' physical traits as very important.[3] Saul was described as more handsome and a head taller than all others. David was also attractive (see 2 Sam. 14:25–27; 1 Sam. 9:2; 16:18). Despite this, leaders were expected to show humility. Absalom often demonstrated pride, and that derails destiny.

AMNON'S SIN

Many trials occur during our journeys as consequences of decisions. After David's sin with Bathsheba, God said the "sword shall never depart from [his] house" (2 Sam. 12:10). This was true, starting with Amnon until after David died when Solomon ordered his brother's death. The family breakdown involved Absalom. His half-brother, Amnon, was David's first-born and likely heir to the throne (see 1 Kings 2:25; 2 Sam. 3:2). He could've chosen an amazing destiny but instead followed sin's path. David hadn't been a good disciplinarian to his son, so Amnon was used to getting his way. He loved Tamar, Absalom's sister, so much that he became sick. Actually, *love* doesn't describe his feelings. Love is patient, kind, and not self-serving (see 1 Cor. 13:4–5). His actions were far from these descriptions. He ached to have her sexually, but he couldn't. She was his half-sister and a virgin; being with her wasn't acceptable (see 2 Sam. 13:1–2).

Beware: *Of the enemy of lust you're determined to fulfill.*

As his desire burned, his friend and cousin Jonadab asked what was wrong. Jonadab was described as "crafty" (2 Sam. 13:3). Paul would've depicted him as having "cunning craftiness of deceitful plotting" (Eph. 4:14). After hearing Amnon's desire, Jonadab proved his wickedness by suggesting Amnon lie in bed and feign sickness. When David checked on him, he should ask his father to send Tamar to prepare food so he could eat from her hand. Being a young man accustomed to getting his way, Amnon liked this plan and petitioned his dad. David should have known his son was devising evil, but he did as Amnon asked. While he was in bed, Tamar made his food, but he refused to eat. He sent everyone away and then asked Tamar to bring it to his bedroom. When she did, he took hold of her hand and asked her to lie with him. She refused, saying that was a disgrace, not the sort of thing done in Israel. If she complied, she'd have nowhere she could go because she'd be considered a fool. Amnon persisted. She said if he asked their dad, he'd give her to Amnon, but he didn't desire her God's way. Amnon wanted what he wanted, so he overpowered and raped her. Then he hated her even more than he'd desired her and sent her away (see Lev. 18:9; 2 Sam. 13:3–15).

Beware: *Of those who want their own desires despite effects on others.*

Tamar's heart was broken by this violation then rejection. Before she left, she told Amnon that his rejecting her was worse than the rape. He told his servant to put her out and lock the door. She tore her many-colored robe, a garment for the king's virgin daughters. She put ashes on her head, laid her hand on her head, and wept bitterly. Absalom realized what had happened, confirmed Amnon's actions, and despised his brother. Though his anger seethed, he didn't confront Amnon immediately but resolved to exact revenge on his beloved sister's behalf. He told Tamar to stay silent because he had vengeance in mind. She lived desolately in his house. His inaction demonstrates his selfishness. Though he understood how devastating this event had been for her, he was more interested in retribution than alleviating her pain (see 2 Sam. 13:16–20). Even while upholding her honor, he thought of his needs—to punish Amnon.

Disobedience to God's law changes us and our families. David reaped what he sowed when he'd connived about Uriah's death. Amnon and Absalom both turned out to be schemers. When David was informed about the attack, as king, he should've applied God's law to Amnon's sin. Instead, he was angry but did nothing (see Sam. 13:21). Maybe he balked at dealing with Amnon because of his own sexual sin. Perhaps this again exemplified his poor discipline of his sons. Whatever his reason, he didn't make Amnon accountable. If he had, the end result with Absalom could've been different. As a leader, often no action is worse than the wrong action.

Beware: *Of those who passively fume with hatred that demands fulfillment.*

VENGEANCE

No matter how we plot sweet retaliation, it will turn out bitter because vengeance belongs to God (see Rom. 12:19). Absalom's devious, patient plotting was demonstrated as he bided his time until an opportunity arose. Two years after Amnon's attack, during sheep-shearing time, he invited his brothers, the king, and his servants. David declined; if he'd gone, perhaps this murder wouldn't have occurred. Absalom asked David to send Amnon with the other sons. At first, the king questioned why he wanted Amnon to go, but he ultimately relented (see 2 Sam 13:23–27). David should've followed his instincts. Surely, he realized Absalom's character longed for revenge and lusted for power. His killing Amnon, David's oldest, would put Absalom in line for the throne. He was willing to slay his brother to usurp the eldest's destiny.

Beware: *Of those who deceive so they can destroy.*

Absalom told servants to watch until Amnon was drunk. When he was ready, he'd give the order to kill him. Servants complied; Amnon was slain, and the king's other sons fled. News traveled to David that Absalom had killed all his sons. He tore his clothes and lay on the ground while servants stood with torn garments. After that, Jonadab, David's nephew who'd counseled Amnon to commit the heinous act, told David that only Amnon was dead and that murder was pre-determined since Tamar's rape. His complicity in the rape was compounded by his not having revealed Absalom's plot for vengeance. He informed the king that his other sons were coming back. As they tearfully returned, Absalom fled from his dad to his grandfather, King Talmai. David mourned not only for Amnon but also Absalom. Even though Absalom had killed his firstborn, David longed to see him but was comforted about Amnon's death (see 2 Sam. 13:28–39).

Beware: *Of those who give counsel for problems they caused.*

SETTING UP THE REBELLION

Absalom had lived in Geshur for three years, likely pampered by his grandfather. Now, he wanted to come home. David longed to see him; so because of Joab's concern for David, he manipulated him into approving Absalom's return. However, no reconciliation occurred between father and son. David said Absalom could go to his own house but not see his dad. They both had responded wrong concerning Amnon's death. However, neither apologized, talked, or made amends for his part. David must've known Absalom's punishment wasn't sufficient for his crime since he didn't see his son for two additional years. Absalom grew restless. Twice, he asked Joab to arrange a meeting, but Joab didn't respond. Because he didn't answer his bidding, Absalom again showed his vindictive side and sent servants to burn Joab's barley fields. After Joab confronted him, Absalom insisted he approach David and ask why he refused to see his son. He claimed staying in Geshur would've been better. He wanted to see David; but if he had iniquity in him, he wanted to be executed. The enemy frequently uses that type of statement to appeal to our emotions, but manipulation is a trait that makes us unfit for the destiny God has planned. David responded just how Absalom knew he would. He agreed to his demands. When Joab relayed the message, David called for Absalom, who came and bowed before him. David then kissed him (see 2 Sam. 13:38–39; 14:1, 21–24, 28–33). A peaceful reunion, however, wasn't Absalom's end game.

Beware: *Of treacherous ones who are suddenly contrite.*

Before and after we've arrived at destiny, our insidious enemy tries shrewdly to steal what God's given. Like he'd patiently plotted his revenge on Amnon, Absalom spent his years in banishment concocting a takeover scheme. His reasons for wanting to take by force what would have probably been his someday aren't stated. Perhaps he held bitterness about his three-year banishment to Geshur, followed by two more years of estrangement. He'd probably harbored resentment toward his father for about a decade for not chastising Amnon. He may have still seethed about David's affair with Bathsheba—wife, daughter, and granddaughter of close family friends. Because he was several years older than Solomon, he undoubtedly experienced normal sibling rivalry or may have resented David's attention to his younger son. He also likely knew Solomon was God's choice for the nation's next king because God had sent the prophet Nathan to name Solomon after he was born (see 2 Sam.

12:25). Cultivating unforgiveness hurts destiny, and it negated Absalom's chances to be king.

Absalom used this opportunity to deceive David and win the kingdom. He assembled chariots, horses, and fifty men to go before him. He rose early each morning and stood beside the gate to ensure anyone with a lawsuit would approach him instead of the king. He was pleasing, endearing, good-looking, and accommodating. He charmed people through these interactions and influenced and wooed them while maligning David. He said David had no deputy to hear grievances; if Absalom were made judge, he'd give justice. He won Israel's hearts (see 2 Sam. 15:1–6, 13). This was again manipulation, and "those who are such do not serve our Lord Jesus Christ, but their own belly, and by smooth words and flattering speech deceive the hearts of the simple" (Rom. 16:18). David had manipulated Uriah. Now that technique was used against him.

Beware: *Of those who endear themselves to others to undermine leadership.*

After four years, Absalom asked to go to Hebron to repay a vow he'd made while in Geshur—to serve the Lord if he were allowed to return to Jerusalem. Actually, the trip was part of his overthrow plot. Hebron was Absalom's birthplace; he probably had friends there or knew some who resented David's moving the capital to Jerusalem after he ruled the whole nation. The king gave Absalom permission, so he exploited this ruse. He sent spies throughout Israel, saying when they heard the trumpet sound, they'd know Absalom reigned in Hebron. He took 200 men unaware of his intentions. He also sent for David's counsellor, Ahithophel. The conspiracy grew, and more people joined Absalom's ranks. When David heard Absalom had won many hearts, he told his people to flee while they could. Servants vowed allegiance to David; so he and his household fled, except for ten concubines. David, barefoot and with his head covered, traveled to the Mount of Olives and wept. Others also covered their heads and cried (see 2 Sam. 15:7–16, 30). Sometimes we should stand and fight, but sometimes our best defense is to run and let God protect destiny.

Beware: *Of those who will turn against you to follow a duplicitous one.*

BROOK KIDRON

While fleeing his traitorous son, "The king himself also crossed over the Brook Kidron" (2 Sam. 15:23). As he did, this man was experiencing one of the hardest times of his destiny journey. His grandson, many generations later, would deal with the same dynamics, in the same place. Jesus "went out with His disciples over the Brook Kidron, where there was a garden, which He and His disciples entered" (John 18:1). Gethsemane had been His refuge for rest, prayer, and time with His Father. However, instead of His sanctuary, that night Jesus dealt with much after He crossed the Kidron. Earlier, He'd demonstrated humility as He broke bread and washed the feet of those who'd later be disloyal. Afterward, all His group would desert Him (see John 13:4-5; Mk. 14:50). Like David was betrayed by his beloved son, Jesus would be handed over by one of his select men.

He dreaded His impending, ultimate, destiny fulfillment and prayed intensely for God's will, but "if it [were] possible, [to] let this cup pass" (Matt. 26:39). Like David and his companions wept as they fled from Absalom, Jesus prayed loudly and tearfully with such stress that "His sweat became like great drops of blood falling" (Luke 22:44). Three times he asked God to change His assignment. However, although He understood what was to happen, He still showed love. While Judas kissed Him, Jesus called him, "Friend" (Matt. 26:49–50). During His Kidron time, Jesus was harassed and troubled. Though David's Lord was sorrowful as He experienced Kidron, He returned triumphantly over death. Though David was shattered as he crossed the Kidron, he returned victoriously over rebellion.

Beware: *Of thinking struggles are more than you can bear.*

THE END

As predetermined, Hushai sent David information about Absalom's strategies through priests. A female servant passed it along through two of David's men, Ahimaaz and Jonathan. They told him not to stay in the plains that night but to cross the Jordan. The men attempted to avoid being spotted by not going into the city but staying in En Rogel. However, they were recognized by a boy, who informed Absalom. They escaped to a man's house and hid in a well while a woman spread a covering and grain over it. When Absalom's servants approached, she said they'd gone over the brook. They searched, then returned to Jerusalem. David's men left the well to tell David to escape quickly because Ahithophel had counseled against him. David and his entourage crossed the Jordan and were gone by morning when Absalom and his men crossed. This allowed David to set up in Mahanaim, where loyal followers brought food and supplies to replenish him and his men. David divided his people into thirds and set captains over them. When he said he'd go to battle with them, they adamantly opposed. If they were defeated in battle, no one would care; but David would be worth 10,000 of them. They asked him to go instead to the city. He deferred to them but instructed his captains to be kind to Absalom (see 2 Sam. 17:15–22, 24, 28–29; 18:1–5). Everyone heard that order, but some didn't obey.

Beware: *Of those who ignore leadership's directives.*

The two factions fought in the woods of Ephraim, and David's army overthrew them. As many as 20,000 of Absalom's Israelites were killed that day, mostly by the woods' rugged terrain. While escaping on a mule, Absalom rode beneath thick, tree branches. His hair caught; but the mule continued, leaving Absalom suspended above the ground. How ironic that one source of Absalom's great pride—his hair—had led to his downfall. In keeping with his proud nature, he'd erected a pillar to celebrate his destiny arrival in the same conceited way Saul had done years before when God stripped the kingdom from him (see 2 Sam. 18:6–9, 18; 1 Sam. 15:12). David's son with charisma, intelligence, and potential had squandered his destiny. As he hung suspended above the rocky terrain, I wonder if he regretted his decision to kill Amnon or still felt justified. Maybe he cried out for God's mercy as he struggled to free himself from certain death if David's men found him. Perhaps, even when his demise loomed as a reality, he inwardly chuckled, still haughty and assured his dad would protect him like always. Maybe he considered the irony of erecting himself a monument only to end with this ignoble death. A few days before, as he conspired against his dad, he was full of dreams about his grand destiny.

Now his legacy would be dangling from a tree. God's purpose and plan will come to pass.

When someone told Joab that Absalom was hanging helplessly, Joab asked why he hadn't killed him. He said he would've given him ten shekels of silver and a belt to do that. The man said he wouldn't have killed Absalom for 1,000 because he was the king's son. He reminded Joab of David's admonishment that no one was to hurt Absalom. Joab and his armor bearers found the helpless Absalom and stabbed him. Not long after his insurrection, Absalom was dead. They put his body into a pit and covered it with rocks. Instead of being a great Israeli king with a monument to memorialize him, Absalom died with no son to perpetuate his name and was buried beneath a pile of rocks (see 2 Sam. 18:10–18).

Beware: *Of pride and arrogance that will be your demise.*

TAKING THE MESSAGE

Ahimaaz asked Joab if he could tell David about the battle. Instead, Joab asked the Cushite to run to David. Ahimaaz again asked Joab to let him go because he was faster. After Joab gave permission, Ahimaaz outran the Cushite and approached David as he sat between two gates. When the watchman told David someone was coming, he recognized Ahimaaz. David said he was a good man. Known for his running abilities, Ahimaaz had been responsible for delivering messages to David during the uprising. Ahimaaz called out, "All is well" (2 Sam. 18:28) and told David that God had delivered the enemy into their hands. However, when David asked about Absalom, Ahimaaz said he saw a tumult but didn't know the cause (see 2 Sam. 15:36; 18:19–29). This story says much. Some seem like the best choice to carry the message, but maturity is required to run the race quickly and with a relevant word.

Beware: *Of those who are swifter but have nothing significant to communicate.*

The Cushite arrived and informed David that Absalom was dead, so the king retired to the chamber above the gate and mourned. His grief was typical for a parent who lost a child. Absalom had acted like his enemy.

He'd slyly plotted then slain his older brother. He sought to take over his dad's kingdom then kill him. He'd lain with David's concubines. However, when he died, David wasn't thinking about his son's tarnished past but was consumed with heartache. He probably acknowledged his responsibility for Absalom's character and that his lack of discipline led to his son's flaws. Maybe he grasped that Nathan's prophecy about consequences for his sins against Uriah had come true. Now, Absalom wasn't his enemy, just his beloved son. He probably remembered his little boy born in Hebron. While he was learning to walk as the king of Judah, his son was learning to walk in life. He surely recalled times when Absalom hugged him closely and vowed his love for his daddy or recollected the scent of his son's thick hair. Now, David had lost that son, and he wished he'd died instead. His grief made him react from emotions, not as Israel's king. After Joab cautioned him about his extreme grief, David moved to the city's gate, the place of authority, and sat so people could approach him (see 2 Sam. 18:32–33; 19:5–8). Sometimes our destiny positions mean we must keep leading though our heart aches.

Beware: *Of overwhelming emotions that cripple and cloud leadership ability.*

David attempted to soothe hurt accompanying Absalom's uprising. He promised that Amasa, also his nephew, would be leader of the army, not Joab. David's reasoning for promoting him wasn't stated, but perhaps he thought he'd secure Absalom's followers' allegiance since Amasa had led Absalom's army. He may have wanted to punish Joab for killing his son. He also dealt with other issues from the uprising. David had been the victor, but some complained about him. Though he'd delivered them from enemies, especially the Philistines, he'd fled from Absalom. Others were questioning why elders weren't bringing David back as king. David sent priests to ask Judah's leaders why they were last to want him back when all Israel wanted him. After he reminded them that they were related, elders asked him to return. Then, men of Israel and Judah quarreled about who had more entitlement to the king and bantered fierce words (see 2 Sam. 19:9–14, 42-43). David certainly had dealt with these types of disagreements among his strong-willed boys.

Beware: *Of vengeance from one who's supplanted from his or her place of rank.*

CONCLUSION

Destiny journeys are fraught with those desperately desiring our callings. Sometimes even loved ones. David said, "Those who seek my life, to destroy it, shall go into the lower parts of the earth [and] fall by the sword;...but the mouth of those who speak lies shall be stopped" (Ps. 63:9–11). By protecting us, the Father protects the destiny He created for us.

DAVID'S WEAPONS: TRIALS

———

DAVID'S REFLECTIONS

In my distress I called upon the LORD, and cried out to
my God; He heard my voice from His temple, and my cry
came before Him, even to His ears. (Ps. 18:6)

A difficult but crucial part of destiny preparation is trials. We're not promised
an easy road but rather are to *expect* suffering and hardships (see John 16:33).
Jesus said He chose and appointed us to bear fruit, but our vine must be pruned
periodically to accomplish that (see John 15:16, 2). Pruning comes through
trials, an amazing growth tool for faith, character, knowledge, perseverance.
Satan wants to steal the promise and derail our mission, so he sends vicious
trials. Some come because we stand for Jesus' name, and with that trial comes
blessing. Other times, they're consequences for our actions, such as being "a
murderer,…thief,…evildoer, or…busybody in other people's matters" (1 Pet.
4:15). Then, God allows trouble because of His love—so we can change. Often,
though, trials come because of our calling and potential. Solomon said if you
have oxen, you should expect messes (see Prov. 14:4). In other words, if you're
doing something to enhance the kingdom, your life won't be without trials.

Beware: *Of thinking trials are punishments from God instead of His tool for
promotion.*

Isaiah describes testing as the "furnace of affliction," "bread of adversity
and the water of affliction" (Isa. 48:10; 30:20). That says much. Fire and
hardships build faith, a greater gift than precious metals, which perish
in fire while faith grows (see 1 Pet. 1:7). Trials heat things up like with
the Three Hebrew Children, thrown into the furnace because of their
commitment to God (see Dan. 3:19). As much as we'd love to be delivered
from our trial, sometimes God doesn't rescue us *from* that furnace but
allows us to remain *in* it where He stays with us as He purifies us into gold
and silver. While trials occur, we don't see how we're changing but know
they're uncomfortable. We may wonder where God is or question if the

trials will ever end. If God has left us or sees our attacks. If our promise will ever come to fruition. Even Jesus questioned during His ordeal: "My God, My God, why have You forsaken Me?" (Matt. 27:46). God's always there, and His plan isn't to make us defeated, but rather to make us defeaters. In the meantime, we stay the course so trials promote rather than demote. Don't despise battles because victories come after battles.

God allows tribulation to create traits for us to be destiny-ready. David learned that lesson. He endured brokenness, desperation, hardship, and healing before he was king. During his nearly two decades from calling to kingship, he certainly must've eagerly awaited his tenure. However, he had to stay focused while responding with integrity and respect for Israel's current king. Throughout the trials' severity, he learned and grew because he was confident that, "The Lord [would] perfect that which concern[ed him]" (Ps. 138:8). We just keep on, keepin' on and don't let trials become distractions from what the Lord is perfecting in us. We continue to walk worthy of His calling (see Eph. 4:1). David understood that victories belong to the Lord, and setbacks would refine and prepare him for God's purpose.

Beware: *Of letting trials discourage and make you give up.*

ADULLAM

While on Saul's hit list, David departed from Gath and escaped to the cave of Adullam, one spot exemplifying a low point in his journey. When his brothers and those of his father's house heard, they joined him (see 1 Sam. 22:1). A few years before, Jesse's house was honored by the king because of David's slaying the giant. Now, likely the whole family was in this dismal cave because of David's calling. Often, even extended family is affected when we answer the Lord's call. Circumstances shift during destiny journeys, and our path may seem to be veering the opposite direction from our promise. We may find ourselves in a dark cavern where we can't even see our hand, let alone our direction. However, no matter how things appear, God's purpose remains sure, and *He* never loses sight of our destinies.

David asked the Moabite king if his parents could stay until he ascertained God's will. That detail shows his growth in seeking the Lord, plus his honor and love for his parents. Moab had been the home of Ruth,

David's great-grandmother. Although Moabites were Israel's enemies, David likely had family connections. After he left his parents, he returned to Adullam (see 1 Sam. 22:3–4). Everyone in that cave, was a mess—those "in distress...debt, and...discontented gathered to him" (1 Sam. 22:2). David became captain of those 400 misfit men. During this great trial, he probably had uncertainties, but God had a plan for everyone in the cave. Our destinies entwine with others who are on their own voyages to God's purpose. In our dark, dank Adullams, we should seek God about where we go from there. It's in dark places that God gives clear vision, With the Lord's revelations, we can reassess, repent, renew, realign, or rest.

Beware: *Of thinking your current situation will never change.*

Even though things seemed bleak, David wrote while in the cave: "O Lord...You are my refuge, my portion in land of living" (Ps. 142:5). No matter the trial, regardless of how musty the cave, or how long they stayed, God was his portion. Saul's persecution worked for David's good, just like for First Century disciples. Because of persecution, they scattered from Jerusalem and spread Jesus' message abroad (see Acts 8:1). David's experiences would ultimately affect his and his men's destinies. Adullam, meaning "their testimony,"[1] teaches that trials become testimonies to encourage others. How often has another's testimony blessed and reassured us? We should "count it all joy" in our Adullams (James 1:4). Adverse situations will change and later testify of God's infinite love. God did a work in everyone in that cave. These Adullam misfits became David's mighty men of valor. He can also use our Adullams to prepare us misfits as His mighty army.

Beware: *Of wasting experiences that could mold you into a mighty man or woman of valor.*

ZIKLAG

A while later David and his men had been living in Philistia at Ziklag. There, they were safe from Saul while God did more work among David's entourage. After Philistine leaders refused to let him go to battle against Israel, David and his men returned to Ziklag. Then, another great trial occurred that made him fall even lower than at Adullam. Amalekites had burned their city and taken everything—possessions, wives, children. Can you imagine that group's sense of futility? They were mentally and physically exhausted after avoiding Saul for years then living among the Philistines, who hated them. Now, everything that mattered was ravaged. As they surveyed their homes routed by the Amalekites, hope they'd carried all these years of being part of God's plan, dissipated. Devastated by massive losses and circumstances that looked opposite of God's promised destiny, they "wept, until they had no more power to weep" (1 Sam. 30:4). This sorrow deepened when David's men, faithful during hardest times, blamed him and intended to stone him. In reality, David's decision to stay in the Philistine land then raid nearby nations probably *did* contribute to the Ziklag tragedy (see 1 Sam. 30:1–6; 27:8). His grief over their calamity was probably even more profound because of his feelings of guilt.

Even in this hard trial, David knew where strength lay. During earlier bad times, he'd acted without God's direction, but now he took his struggles to Him. He received guidance to pursue the Amalekites. They attacked and defeated them, while retrieving more than was stolen. But God wasn't finished blessing David. Because Saul had died, David could probably go back safely, so he inquired of God. With the Lord's direction, David and his men took their families and lived in Hebron. There, days after his darkest point, God established him as king when Judah's men rejected Ishbosheth (see 1 Sam. 30:7–8, 17–20; 2 Sam. 2:1–4). His becoming Judah's king demonstrates an important warfare concept—Before Morning Nautical Twilight (BMNT). Soldiers know that before dawn is the darkest and most common time for enemy attack. Daylight's on the way, but everything's blackest right before it comes. Sometimes greatest victories come after worst defeats, because the enemy's fighting to make us surrender before triumph. A few days before, David was a defeated shepherd boy turned warrior. Now, he was king of Judah, one step closer to God's plan.

Beware: *Of conceding defeat after the enemy's worst attack.*

During Adullam and Ziklag, Scripture doesn't say what David did each day to receive direction, encouragement, and renewed purpose. He probably prayed and sought God's will for him and his men. God was faithful and had a reason for

David's despair. Despite the Ziklag devastation, Amalekites didn't kill anyone (see 1 Sam. 30:2). In addition, David grew into a man who sought the Lord's will. While it happened, they likely weren't thinking they were where God wanted them because He had bigger plans. Often we feel God's deserted us (see Ps. 22:1–2), but later we see how adversities worked into His purpose. What's God doing in hard times for, to, and through you—respect for authority, humility, trust, obedience, integrity? Will you come from Adullam and Ziklag knowing He's in control and growing you up toward His plan?

WEALTH

The message is clear—don't despise hardships but rather delight in them because of the wealth they produce in you (see Rom. 5:3–4). David understood that wealth came the hard way. In one of my favorite scriptures, the psalmist said, "Before I was afflicted I went astray, but now I keep Your word" (Ps. 119:67). Trials are God's utter love as He purges what could hinder us from moving further into our callings. Hardships yield wealth while eliminating undesirable issues—gossip, unforgiveness, negativity, anger, self-centeredness. Trials teach what good times don't, so we grow or eliminate what could influence destiny. How we react during trials determines how long we're in them or if we move into our next season.

Peter is a great example of growth. He had unclean lips, talked out of turn, denied Jesus, was called satan by Jesus. Yet Peter grew into someone who could walk on water and whom Jesus called a rock. Judas was also one of only twelve men who knew Jesus like none other before or since. He walked and talked with the Lord personally but had character flaws that never changed. His avarice was displayed as the ministry treasurer when he stole money from their ministry box then betrayed Jesus for silver. While Peter's destiny was to be a great part of the First Century church, Judas' destiny was in a field where he hanged himself (see John 12:4–6; Matt. 26:14–15; 27:5). Preparing for destiny involves trials and tests to grow us up and clean us up. Through and because of trials, David gained wealth that produced his arsenal of weapons necessary to reign.

Suffering isn't a bad thing when we hurt for doing good things rather than evil (see 1 Pet. 3:17). We should be glad for His refining because He sees something of value in us—enough to give a repeat course when we fail. Our attitude should be "rejoicing in hope, patient in tribulation" (Rom. 12:12). As much as that doesn't make sense, hard times should make us rejoice. Precious jewels evolve from pressure: diamonds (coal), rubies (rocks), and sapphires (lava). Pearls are born through adversity as debris is planted in an oyster. Its nacre becomes the shell and inside lining. Layer-upon-layer covers the irritant and produces a more valuable pearl. That covering is called the pearl's mantle.[2] Our mantle—our calling—is our covering, too. Let rains pelt, winds blow, and multiple layers of adversity cover us, the LORD will deliver those He's called. Trust and faith are strengthened as we observe His faithfulness.

How do we wounded warriors in our Adullams go from debris to pearl, from called to chosen? Like a long journey creates the pearl, "We must through many tribulations enter the kingdom" (Acts 14:22). David grew through each hardship: a lion; bear; giant; demons; war with hostile nations; sibling rivalry; sons' betrayals; demonic king who took his wives, betrayed, pursued, and aspired to murder him. Though at times he wondered if God had forgotten him (see Ps. 13:1), he knew God was his Provider and Source of victory. Adullam and Ziklag seasons brought forth the extraordinary in David and his men. What's the extraordinary God's birthing in you during adversities in your destiny journey?

AMMON

One of David's trials after he was king of Israel stemmed from a personal attack against his men. Although the earlier event is unclear, at some point during Saul's pursuit, Nahash (king of Ammon) assisted David (the fugitive). Men named Nahash were mentioned several times. David's half-sister, Abigail, was the daughter of his mother and Nahash. Shobi, son of Nahash of Rabbah, brought supplies to David when he fled from Absalom. Saul rejected King Nahash's proposal for Israel to put out their right eyes (see 2 Sam. 17:25, 27; 1 Sam. 11:2). If this was the same Nahash, this event with Saul may have been why Nahash had shown kindness to David during Saul's persecution. Historians aren't sure if any of these are the correct man or what event sparked David's compassion.

In whatever way Nahash showed kindness, after his death, his son

Hanun reigned. David (now Israel's king) wanted to pay his respects. He sent servants to comfort Hanun, but Ammonite princes told Hanun that David had sent them to spy (see 2 Sam 10:1–3). During our destiny journeys and once we arrive, we need good counselors. Flattering, flowery, deceptive guidance doesn't benefit us. Instead, godly, mature wisdom—even a hard word—helps us make godly, mature decisions. David's grandson, King Rehoboam, would discover that principle. When he required guidance, he asked his father's counselors and then his younger, less-seasoned advisers. Choosing guidance from young men or mentors of the wisest man ever should've been easy. However, he chose his friends' words and lost most of his kingdom. The first scripture in Psalms says a man is blessed when he doesn't act on ungodly counsel (see 1 Kings 12:8, 16–17; Ps. 1:1). Rehoboam's not heeding sage advice negatively altered his and his children's destinies.

Beware: *Of leadership that seeks counsel then doesn't choose well.*

King Hanun chose badly also. To prove David's servants were spies, he shaved off half their beards; cut their garments to the buttocks; and sent them away, violated, insulted, and humiliated (see 2 Sam. 10:4). Because Hebrew men didn't wear pants beneath their robes,[3] this act exposed their nakedness and circumcision to heathens. It also challenged their manhood. They were shamed and debased by unfair actions that occurred just because their king had sent them on a mission. Doesn't that sound like the enemy's treatment? He twists our kindness to bring disgrace, but he doesn't have the last word. Though at the time all we can see is hurt, those trials are a sign that the King has called and chosen us for His purpose. American author Stephen Mansfield said it this way: "The confirmation of history is that we are not called despite our wounding and betrayal; we are wounded and betrayed because we are called. And God yearns to make your pain redemptive in your life."[4] The Father's going to use this for something greater for the kingdom. Hanun's contemptuous act was against the king's emissaries, so it was also against King David. When we represent the King, He represents us. What hurts us, hurts Him. Attacks against us are personal to our King, and He will vindicate.

Beware: *Of those who assault or humiliate the King's representatives.*

When King David heard about the atrocity, he cared for his men's dignity and honor. He left the city to meet and spare them the humiliation of returning to Jerusalem. He allowed them to "wait at Jericho until [their] beards ha[d] grown, and then return" (2 Sam. 10:1–5). This showed his character and love for his people. He tended to their well-being and offered an oasis. What a beautiful picture of our King's tenderness! When we're devastated, He comes to where we are. He loves us and everything that matters to us, even something as insignificant as our beards. David once said those who hated him were "more than the hairs of [his] head" (Ps. 69:4). Our hair is important to the Lord, whether He's counting what we've lost on the bathroom floor or acknowledging enemies who rise against us (see Luke 12:7). If God numbers our enemies like he numbers our hair, He knows what affects us at all times. He's interested in every aspect of our walk with Him and each occurrence in our lives. If everything is significant, think about His reaction to vicious attacks because we're doing His work.

LET THEM BE ASHAMED

I wonder if David thought of his servants when he said, "Let no one who waits on You be ashamed; let those be ashamed who deal treacherously without cause" (Ps. 25:3). God can use anything to produce His will—an ass' jawbone, a great fish, our worst enemy. Jeremiah later said: "Surely I will cause the enemy to intercede with you in the time of adversity and… affliction" (Jer. 15:11). God sometimes allows us to be wounded to bring forth something greater in preparation for destiny. Those Ammonite actions allowed God to show Himself mighty on Israel's behalf and spelled defeat for Ammon. Hanun realized David despised them for this outrage and would retaliate. To prepare, the Ammonites hired a great army with chariots and horsemen from Mesopotamia; 22,000 Syrians; 32,000 chariots and 1,000 men from the king of Maacah; and 12,000 men from Ish-Tob (see 2 Sam. 10:6). Numbers in this massive army were not superior to God. If the King assigns vengeance, they can hire all the armies they want, but they won't prevail.

Beware: *Of your reaction of fear when enemies assemble against you.*

We should war to the best of our ability but know victory ultimately comes from God (see Prov. 21:31). As Ammonites gathered, David sent Joab and his mighty men to answer the growing army. The Ammonites emerged in battle array to the city's entrance while allies were stationed in the field. As this huge army attacked, Israel defeated the Syrians and Ammorites, who became their servants (see 2 Sam. 10:7–9, 18–19). David said something Jesus repeated: "Sit...till [the Lord] make[s] Your enemies Your footstool" (Ps. 110:1; Matt. 22:44). If enemies are under our feet, why do we let them inside our heads so often? Refuse satan and say, "You ain't the boss of me." Let them be ashamed!

OUR BROTHERS

Many assume the worst about those fulfilling an assignment for the King. Wounding doesn't always happen by enemy hands, but by brothers who attack, often because of our assignments. David experienced assaults more than once by his natural and Hebrew brothers. When he picked up stones at the brook during the Goliath encounter, he could've justifiably flung them at those brothers. Saul would shortly begin his persecution; and Eliab, David's oldest brother, had just insulted him *again*. However, David knew his brothers weren't the enemy but that the true adversary loomed gigantically in front of him. Satan's "the accuser of [the] brethren" (Rev. 12:10). The phrase, "of the brethren," is interesting. Often accusations come not from unbelievers but from brothers or sisters against brothers or sisters, by satan's design. He deploys whomever or whatever he can to accuse and divide. When brothers and sisters are chosen for God's purpose, we shouldn't attack but rejoice. We're all part of the same army.

Abner once told Joab to stop chasing his brethren. Too often even God's generals pursue brothers, not enemies. Once when God was angry with Judah, Israel and Syria waged war against them. They killed 120,000 men of Judah and captured women and children (see 2 Chron. 28:5–8). God sent the prophet Oded to tell of His anger about Israel's actions against Judah, whom they "killed...in a rage that reache[d] ...heaven" (2 Chron. 28:9). If we devastate brothers, that action reaches heaven, and we'll suffer consequences. Hurts will happen, but God will take vengeance upon whoever causes the offense. More than "all things[,] have fervent love for one another, for 'love will cover a multitude of sins'" (1 Pet. 4:8). Loving our brothers makes us want them to succeed, not be beaten down by our words or actions.

Beware: *Of those who treat brothers as an enemy to be destroyed.*

This reminds me of a group of ladies who met with other Christians who had something in common—they couldn't conceive. They wanted children as part of their journeys, so they became friends and rejoiced as group members became pregnant one-by-one. They could've grown envious but understood that as they reacted joyfully for each other, their turn would come. And it did. Birthing destiny is the same. Many don't celebrate when someone is on business for the King but instead react in envy, self-centeredness, or other ugly ways David's enemies did. Instead of jubilation, those people seek annihilation of one who births God's calling. We can be envious as we see others stepping into their destinies, or we can rejoice. Celebrate! Our turn will come.

Beware: *Of those who forget the true enemy and persecute brothers instead.*

FOR A SEASON

Current situations don't negate our being created as warriors to dwell in Jerusalem. Adullam, Ziklag, or Jericho didn't transform David's men into weaklings. However, sometimes we require a season of rest to be whole again. How do we go from hopeless to hopeful? From cowering in the cave of despair to stepping up as mighty men and women of valor? While in Adullam David wrote, "When my spirit was overwhelmed…You knew my path" (Ps. 142:3). He knows! Today's circumstances may seem devastating, but trust Him. He'll lead us through that trial and use it as a destiny path. However, we can't take up long-term residence there. When Israel exited Egypt, God said "to go forward" (Exod. 14:15). Don't become stationary or look behind, but go forward toward His plan. I once heard a speaker say even if you fall, fall forward. In Adullam, the prophet Gad came and said, "Do not stay in the stronghold; depart" (1 Sam. 22:5). David's men retreated for a season, but eventually they had to go forward. Rise in faith from dire circumstances, your Adullam. Trials are to go through, not to stay in.

Beware: *Of becoming comfortable in what's familiar.*

David said his servants could wait *until* their beards grew "then return" (2 Sam. 10:5). The king didn't say, *maybe* or *if*. Recovery is temporary, and we *will* grow better. David and his mighty men were warriors to go forth into battle rather than wallow in hardships. As we become stronger, we'll rise from those circumstances. Gideon couldn't stay in the winepress if he were to accomplish the greatness God had planned for this mighty warrior and judge. Hannah had to get up after her word from Eli so she could become impregnated and birth God's plan for her and Israel (see Judg. 6:12; 8:28; 1 Sam. 1:18). However, during fragile seasons, the Lord's servants can rest without guilt or condemnation. The King not only said it's okay, but it was His idea. We'll emerge from Jericho, Adullam, and Ziklag stronger and renewed. Our King sympathizes because He endured trials like ours (see Heb. 4:15). What could we suffer that He doesn't understand? Like King David and his men experienced wounding, so did King Jesus. *His* nakedness was exposed; *His* beard, plucked out. *He* was mocked, criticized, lied about, slapped, beaten, spat upon, wounded, and crucified. He's been there, done that. He permits these seasons because something's happening to complete one more step toward becoming destiny-ready.

CONCLUSION

Tribulation didn't happen exclusively to David, Jesus, or us. David understood that trials would take him one step closer to his destiny, but adversities didn't stop once he became king—Philistines, a daughter's rape by her brother, sons killing sons, son's death by a friend, sons' rebellions, people's hesitation to welcome him back as king. Paul, a man of numerous trials, said, "We are hard-pressed on every side, yet not crushed; we are perplexed, but not in despair; persecuted, but not forsaken; struck down, but not destroyed" (2 Cor. 4:8–9). Therefore, while in trials, we shouldn't pray, "Why me, Lord?" but "Lord, what do You want to change in me?" Through trials, God's refining His gold, His pearls, His diamonds, His workers, His kings.

QUESTIONS TO PONDER
(Answers in Appendix)
ABSALOM

1. Describe Absalom's physical traits.

2a. What was Amnon's sin?

2b. How did Absalom immediately react?

3. How was Absalom under-handed in this matter?

4. Give details of Absalom's banishment and return.

6. How did Absalom endear himself to Israel?

7. How did pride contribute to Absalom's death?

TRIALS

8. What did Isaiah mean when he spoke of "the furnace of affliction"?

9. Give common descriptions of people hiding at Adullam.

10. What happened at Ziklag?

11. Give examples of wealth gained by trials.

12. Explain what happened at Ammon.

13. What message came from the Prophet Gad?

Something to Consider: How does David's enemy/weapon in this chapter speak about our enemies/weapons today?

Chapter Three

THE PHILISTINES

DAVID'S REFLECTIONS

[When David pretended to be mad at Gath] Evil shall slay the wicked, and those who hate the righteous shall be condemned. The LORD redeems the soul of His servants, and none of those who trust in Him shall be condemned. (Ps. 34:21–22)

The Philistines represent powerful, unbelieving foes who've been around a long time. They often have better resources and seemingly greater power; but they win skirmishes against us, not the war. They were Israel's enemy during much of its history, and David's lifetime was no exception. First discussed in Genesis when Abraham made covenant with Abimelech at Beersheba, Abraham stayed in the Philistine land a while (see Gen. 21:32–34). During David's time they were an extremely rich nation with highly developed city states. With their strong, iron weapons, they were aggressive about invading lands and setting up fortresses to eliminate others' invasions.[1] Their expansion into territories God had promised Israel created conflicts. Whenever God promises you a destiny, the enemy always tries to steal that promise.

THE ARK

When God gives a Promised Land, territory were to conquer is likely occupied by the enemy. Philistines were a problem since before Saul, and much of his reign was filled with intense war with them. However, the Lord promised to save Israel from them through David's hand (see 2 Sam. 3:18). One event spanned from Eli's years as judge to David's reign. After the Philistines defeated Israel and killed Eli's sons, they stole the Ark of the Covenant. Eli was ninety-eight and couldn't see well. Upon learning about his sons' deaths and the ark's capture, he fell from his seat and broke his neck. The Philistines carried the prized ark to Ashdod at the house of their god, Dagon (see 1 Sam. 4:11, 15, 18; 5:2). Many are interested in having God in their lives, but they also want to keep their idols. Serving two G(g)ods didn't work for the Philistines, nor for us. This theft seemed to be a Philistine victory but ended in defeat.

Beware: *Of those who worship idols but still want God.*

The Philistines likely intensely celebrated their victory and recited the story of the ark's capture, which meant the Hebrew God could no longer ensure Israel's success. However, they didn't comprehend the ark's might. It was the presence of the living God who'd defeat them and their impotent gods. For two consecutive nights, Dagon's statue fell on its face. It broke the second night and left only the torso, so that signaled the end of Ashdod's Dagon worship. However, this wasn't the conclusion of trouble associated with the ark. People in Ashdod and its territories became ravaged with tumors, or "emerods" (1 Sam. 5:6 KJV) (see 1 Sam. 5:3–6). Some believe these were hemorrhoids,[2] while others have suggested these were infected lymph nodes because of a plague due to rat infestation.[3] Even the holiest object ever on earth becomes an enemy if you take what doesn't belong to you—someone else's spouse, money that isn't yours, tithes owed to God, another person's calling.

Beware: *Of believing you can take what's yours without consequences.*

Philistines had heard stories about the Hebrew God's plagues on Egypt, so they understood that His presence illegally in their midst had caused the problems. They wanted it gone, so they carried it to Gath. Great destruction broke out there also, even among the lords, so they sent it to Ekron. Those people likewise became afflicted. Whoever didn't die was heavily tormented with tumors. After having the ark seven months, Philistines were desperate to return it. After they sought priests and mediums to find out the procedure, they loaded it onto a cart along with a trespass offering of five golden tumors and rats in a chest beside the ark. This represented the number of Philistine lords whose territories were affected. They said Israel's God would be appeased and relieve their suffering, so they sent the ark on a new cart drawn by two cows to see which direction it veered. If the cart turned toward Israel's territory, they'd be certain the Hebrew God had caused their troubles. If it didn't turn toward Israel, they'd know chance had brought devastation upon them (see 1 Sam. 5:7–12; 6:1–11).

BACK IN ISRAEL

The cows turned toward Beth Shemesh, the first Hebrew town on the road.[4] People were harvesting when the cart laden with the ark and golden objects stopped at a field. Israelites rejoiced for its return and broke up the cart's wood for a sacrifice. They were probably radically celebrating this miracle. However, like the Philistines, for Beth Shemesh's men, it brought sorrow, not joy. Disregarding God's command, they looked into the ark. God punished them—50,070 were killed. In essence, *they* became the sacrifice. People in Beth Shemesh sent word to Kirjath Jearin to remove it. They transported the ark to Abinadab's house and consecrated his son, Eleazar, to care for it. It remained there until David became king (see 1 Sam. 6:12–15, 19–21; 7:1).

Beware: *Of excitement that causes you to fall into sin.*

After the ark traveled to Abinadab's house, Samuel called Israel to repent and put away foreign gods so God would deliver them from the Philistines. When Philistines learned Israel had gathered, they battled against them at Mizpah. Hebrews grew afraid and cried out to Samuel, who sacrificed. The Philistines attacked, but the Lord answered the assault with thunder. This confused the enemy, so Israel pursued and pushed them back.

God's hand was against the Philistines, so they didn't come against Israel any more during Samuel's days. Cities they'd taken were restored to Israel (see 1 Sam. 7:3–14). When the enemy tries to derail our promise, God will see that it's fulfilled.

SAUL

Samuel, David, Jonathan, and Saul all fought against Philistines. They defeated Saul but not David. After he reigned two years, Saul took his army to fight the Philistines. He kept 2,000 with him and sent 1,000 with Jonathan. After Jonathan attacked a garrison at Geba, the Philistines amassed a huge army: 30,000 chariots, 6,000 horsemen, and warriors like sand of the sea. Saul called people together, but Israel responded fearfully and hid in caves, thickets, rocks, holes, or pits. While facing this massive army, Saul thought he needed to seek God's wisdom himself because Samuel hadn't yet come to sacrifice. After his foolish, unlawful sacrifice, the Philistines surrounded them. Jonathan and his armor bearer killed several Philistines; then the Lord sent an earthquake. Confusion in the Philistine camp made them fight each other. Hebrews who originally supported the Philistines, plus those hiding in the mountains, joined Israel. As Israel's army fought, the Philistines fled. The Lord saved Israel, but fierce war continued with the Philistines during Saul's life (see 1 Sam. 13:1–9; 14:14–15, 21–23, 52).

Beware: *Looking at odds against you rather than that God is for you.*

DAVID AND THE PHILISTINES

David was a force of God's wrath against the Philistines. He encountered their army when he was responsible for Israel's victory through Goliath's defeat. Later, David and his men also killed 200 Philistines and took their foreskins to Saul. As a result, Philistine princes waged fierce war against Israel. After the priests' slaughter at Nob, David was told the Philistines were fighting against Keilah and robbing threshing floors. God directed him to attack; but his men hesitated to war against such a formidable enemy because they were afraid of their own king, Saul. However, although his men were frightened, David asked God if he should fight. God again said to go down, and He'd deliver them to David. He and his men fought Philistines at Keilah, defeated them greatly, and took their livestock (see 1 Sam. 18:27, 30; 23:1–5).

After David left Nob, he escaped from Saul by going to Gath, Goliath's hometown. Scripture doesn't say David sought God's wisdom for this decision. Settling where people hated him for killing their local hero was probably motivated by his desperate fear of Saul, who now represented a greater enemy than staying among Goliath's people. He aligned with Achish, a Philistine king. However, when Achish's servants reminded him about chants comparing David and Saul, he "was very much afraid of Achish" (1 Sam. 21:12). Maybe David realized Achish would understand that this acclaim referred primarily to David's killing massive numbers of Achish's fellow Philistines. David had also witnessed that Saul's reaction to that same praise about David had led to his current avoidance of Saul. To prevent Achish's potentially negative reaction, David pretended to be mad, moved his hand erratically, scratched at the gates, and drooled. Achish was tricked and didn't try to hurt David Apparently, David felt good about his escape because at this time he wrote Psalm 34, glorifying God for protection and deliverance. This connection made Achish a resource later. They left Gath and ended up in Adullam (see 1 Sam. 21:10–15; 22:1).

Beware: *Of possible repercussions from one who resents your accomplishments.*

AFTER ADULLAM

Saul had continually hunted David, who thought he would "perish someday by the hand of Saul" (1 Sam. 27:1). Because David didn't trust Saul, he decided if he again moved into Philistine territory, the king wouldn't pursue. He and his two wives, 600 men, and their households escaped and dwelt there. Saul heard David was in Gath, so he didn't follow. David acted out of fear and sought sanctuary where he'd feigned craziness. David told Achish if he'd found favor, he wanted to live in a small town and be his servant away from Gath because he wasn't worthy to dwell with the king. More likely, he didn't want Achish to see the extent of his raids on neighboring enemies. Achish gave him Ziklag, which subsequently belonged to Judah's kings. David lived there sixteen months while he and his men raided nations inhabiting the land from olden days, including the Amalekites. He attacked and took livestock and killed men and women so they couldn't tell about the raids. When Achish asked where he'd plundered, David misled him so Achish would think he was disloyal to Israel, and Hebrews now hated David (see 1 Sam. 27:1–12). Despite systematically lying to Achish and dwelling in enemy territory, God protected David for his destiny.

PHILISTINE REJECTION

Sometimes in our journeys, we don't recognize that God's protecting our calling. While David lived in Gath, Philistines readied their army for war against Israel. Achish expected David and his men to go with them and be his permanent chief guardian. Before battle, though, Philistine leaders passed by to inspect troops. When they noticed David and his men in the rear, they questioned Achish. He said he'd "found no fault in [David] since he defected to [him]" (1 Sam. 29:3). Obviously, David's attempts to make Achish believe he'd deserted from Israel were successful. The princes angrily refused to let David participate for fear he might turn on them and realign with Saul. They recited the saying about David's military prowess, referring to their lost countrymen's deaths by David's hand. Achish told David he'd dealt uprightly with him, and he observed no fault in him. Interestingly, he swore by the Hebrew God, probably a sign of respect he'd gained for David and his God. However, because the lords didn't want him there, Achish told David to go back to Ziklag the next morning (see 1 Sam. 29:1–10). Although David was upset about their rejection, this was God's hand of protection. That battle was when Saul and his sons were killed. The Lord protects our destinies, even from our own choices.

Beware: *Of your emotions that allow rejection to taint your ability to see God's hand.*

David's Defeat of the Philistines

David reigned seven and a half years as king of Judah. During that time not much war occurred with the Philistines, but rather with Israel. However, when the Philistines heard David was anointed king of all Israel, they relentlessly searched for him (see 2 Sam. 5:5, 17). During the time he'd lived in their land for more than a year, I'm sure he endured both rejection and personal attacks. Sometimes, we coddle the enemy by tolerating his assaults. But a time comes when we must say, "Enough!" His attacks may be minor or brutal; but as long as we allow them, he'll take advantage. Once, I was scheduled to speak at a night service. That morning, I woke up with no voice, and my face was swollen on one side. I was considering having Wade cover for me when I stepped in a low spot in the backyard and twisted *both* ankles. That's when I got angry. Before I hobbled back into the house, I proclaimed that if I had to sit on a stool and whisper into the mic with my big, fat face, I was going to preach that night. By service time, all issues were resolved. Instead of accommodating enemy attacks, we need to take authority and say, "No more!"

Philistines were enemies David had to defeat if he were to rule in his God-designed destiny. He let the Lord lead the battle. After David heard Philistines were deployed in the Valley of Rephaim, he asked the Lord if he should go against them. God said He'd deliver them to David, so Israel defeated them at Baal Perazim. There, David said "the Lord has broken through my enemies...like a breakthrough of water" (2 Sam. 5:20). As they fled, David commanded people to burn Philistine idols they'd taken into battle. The Philistines then gathered again for war in the same valley. This showed their arrogance to think they could defeat David in the same place and same way he'd already trounced them. This time when David asked the Lord if he should go against them, God had a different plan—circle behind them and advance quickly when his army heard the sound of marching in the tops of mulberry trees. After David heard the sound, he attacked and drove them about fifteen miles.[5] Another time, David assaulted the Philistines and took Gath and its towns as well as other nations. Later his men killed Philistia's remaining giants (see 2 Sam. 5:18–21; 1 Chron. 18:1–3; 20:4–8). Enemies of destiny must fall when God leads.

Beware: *Of enemies who will attack the same way after they've been defeated.*

CONCLUSION

David once said, "The righteous cry out, and the LORD hears, and delivers them.... Many are the afflictions of the righteous, but the LORD delivers him out of them all" (Ps. 34:17, 19). Because he heard from the Lord and obeyed, God gave victory often against Philistines. His fame spread into all lands, and God made nations fear him (see 1 Chron. 14:17). As God advances us into destiny, He'll make us victorious over even the most powerful and threatening enemies while bringing favor with men because of His ability working through us.

DAVID'S WEAPONS: WORSHIP

———

DAVID'S REFLECTIONS

I will praise You with my whole heart...I will sing praises to You. I will worship toward Your holy temple, and praise Your name for Your lovingkindness and Your truth. (Ps. 138:1–2)

Honoring our Father with adoration in worship is crucial for destiny preparation. Our tabernacles, our bodies, are the Lord's, and He dwells in our praise and worship (see 1 Cor. 6:19). David called himself the "sweet psalmist of Israel" (2 Sam. 23:1) and demonstrated his love for God by the massive number of psalms he penned. Although others wrote some—among them Solomon, Moses, Asaph—David's credited with composing seventy-three of the 150 psalms.[1] This number demonstrates his heart for worship, relationship with His Father, and desire to be in His presence. Worship should be our lifestyle as we "Sing praises to God!" (Ps. 47:6). To Him alone.

Jesus said, "The hour is coming, and now is, when the true worshipers will worship the Father in spirit and truth" (John 4:23). Those uses of "worship" are *proskuneo*, "to kiss, like a dog licking his master's hand...prostrate oneself in homage."[2] Loving Him unconditionally like a puppy is a beautiful picture. As Holy Spirit worships through us in truth, abandonment, and surrender, we acknowledge the Father is everything—from Provider to Healer. Many times, like before Jesus raised Lazarus, He worshipped (see John 11:41–42). When He "healed many" (Mark 3:10), the use of *healed* is the word *therapeuo*, meaning "to wait upon menially...adore (God)...cure, heal, worship."[3] With even His healing gifts, He worshipped. As we work for God and travel toward destiny, using our gifts as service to others is part of our worship.

WORSHIP AS WARFARE

Worship is an amazing weapon against enemy attacks. God chose Judah, meaning "praise of the Lord,"[4] to lead the way in the wilderness (see Num.

10:14). His great warriors understood praise and worship's power as it preceded warfare. Paul and Silas, for example, had been arrested; instead of bemoaning their fate, they worshipped while in chains. An earthquake shook the prison, loosing everyone's chains, but not one prisoner escaped (see Acts 16:25–28). True worship breaks chains that bind. Sometimes during our journey, we're shackled as the enemy's prisoner, but worship changes ours and others' situations. When King Jehoshaphat fought against three armies, the Lord's method to achieve victory was to call a corporate fast and put worshippers out front. God told Judah to stand still and watch as He fought and saved them. Jehoshaphat and all Jerusalem bowed before the Lord and sang praises "with voices loud and high" (2 Chron. 20:19). Judah was victorious after God created confusion among the enemies, who killed each other. Israel gathered spoil for three days. Worship brings amazing victories and rewards because God hears the worshipper (see 2 Chron. 20:2-3, 17–25; John 9:31).

Though Elijah wasn't considered a warrior, he warred often against the enemy. When he felt alone in the fight, God told him 7,000 hadn't bowed to or kissed Baal. The word for *kiss* is *nashaq,* meaning "to equip with weapons."[5] Whomever we're kissing—the Lord in worship or the enemy—equips us with weapons. When we align with satan, we settle for his armaments; intimacy with the Father furnishes us with His arsenal. Though David's enemies attempted to ensnare him, his heart remained fast upon the Lord, to whom he sang praises (see Ps. 57:6–7). His battle plan was to "call upon the LORD, who is worthy to be praised; so shall I be saved from my enemies" (2 Sam. 22:4). Worship is warfare, important to every facet of our lives. We don't worship to receive blessings, but blessings come because of worship. Great worship brings great breakthrough and trains us in our destiny journeys.

WHEN WE FEEL THE WORST

Worship isn't just for when we're exuberant. The best opportunity is while in the throes of despair because the Lord turns "mourning into dancing… [,] put[s] off…sackcloth[,] and cloth[es us] with gladness" (Ps. 30:11). Sackcloth was worn by those suffering great sorrow. Worship can change deep mourning—attacks against destiny, battles we've lost—into great joy. David intimately knew how effective worship was during hard times. After his first son with Bathsheba died, David saw people whispering and asked about the baby. When they confirmed the death, he arose, washed, anointed himself, changed his clothes, and went to the Lord's house to worship (see 2 Sam. 12:19–20). He felt the worst sorrow of his life—the loss of a child—yet He worshipped. Whenever we're broken-hearted, He comes near (see Ps. 34:18).

Another time, David was devastated because of Absalom's and Ahithophel's betrayals. Yet, he climbed to the mountaintop to worship. After that, his much-needed answer arrived when God sent Hushai. As he was dying, David heard that yet another of his sons had disobeyed his wishes. He didn't wallow in despair but supported Solomon and then worshipped there in his bed (see 2 Sam. 15:31–32; 1 Kings 1:48). Despite how bad our need or painful the hurt, we should worship. That's the last thing our body wants to do during those times, but it helps the most as we don "the garment of praise for the spirit of heaviness" (Isa. 61:3). Habakkuk said he'd rejoice no matter if everything was falling apart (see Hab. 3:18). Asaph, who ministered regularly before the ark, said to "offer to God thanksgiving.... Call upon [Him] in the day of trouble; [He] will deliver" (Ps. 50:14–15). By giving God thanks, we bank victories. When Hebrews and Philistines needed a deliverer, Philistines worshipped Goliath and lost. David worshipped God and won. When evil spirits plagued Saul, David played anointed worship to war against them. Worship takes our minds off our problems and puts it on Him. The answer to sadness, mourning, depression—praise the Lord! Praise and worship are weapons that propel us into destiny.

ALL CREATION

When Pharisees asked Jesus to rebuke those rejoicing and praising Him, He answered, "if these should keep silent, the stones would immediately cry out" (Luke 19:40). All nations, people, creation, even stones and other types of nature were made to worship. That includes the heavens' rejoicing, earth's gladness, seas' roaring, field's jubilation, and trees' joyous singing (see Ps.

86:9; 96:11–12). While David watched his father's sheep, he wrote some of his worship songs, which later became part of the "Psalms." Alone with his sheep, he probably sang, worshipped, wrote love poems to His Father, and danced like fool while the flock looked on. They likely bobbed their heads and called out to their Creator in the heavenlies, their raspy bleats warbling beautiful lyrics of worship because, "Let everything that has breath praise the Lord" (Ps. 150:6).

The ark's story before David was born shows this concept of creation's worship. When the Philistines sent it toward Israel, they said whichever way the cows turned would show God's will. However, the outcome was rigged so the animals would have no incentive to veer toward Israel. Doesn't that sound like the enemy, who seems to be conceding but is actually protecting his own interests while attempting to make us fail? First, they were milk cows that had never been yoked, so they weren't trained to pull. They were also separated from their calves. By nature, the cows should've moved toward their babies (see 1 Sam. 6:7).

They proceeded toward Judah, "lowing as they went" (1 Sam. 6:12). That lowing sound refers to communication between a mother cow and her calf.[6] However, despite their nature and the lowing with their babies, the cows continued. There, they stopped by a "large stone" (1 Sam. 6:14). Hebrews understood the implication of the cattle halting there. A sacrifice, their worship to the Father, was necessary for the miracle of returning the ark.[7] This desire was so central to their natures that even as their calves were pleading, "Don't leave me, Mama," those mother cows were lowing back, "Baby, I gotta go worship the Father." Nature was made to obey and worship God. Worship should be instinctive to us, too. How we adore the Lord with our worship matters as we move into destiny.

Beware: *Of those whose gestures are an attempt for you to fail.*

RETURNING THE ARK

Worship accompanies God's presence as we "continually offer the sacrifice of praise to God" (Heb. 13:15). David sought that perpetual praise when he set up his tabernacle to house the ark and cultivate intimacy with God.

To show his heart, the tabernacle had constant praise and worship (see 1 Chron. 16:37). I wonder if David thought of his tabernacle when he said, "His praise shall continually be in my mouth" (Ps. 34:1). Obed-Edom, where the ark had stayed for three months, and his thirty-eight brothers also became addicted to God's presence and followed it to Jerusalem (see 2 Sam. 6:11; 1 Chron. 16:38). How awesome the Lord's presence became the catalyst for an entire family's destiny!

Years after the Philistines stole the ark, it was still gone, and David wanted to find God's method for transporting it. He'd tried his way, and Uzzah had died. However, his grief didn't become a distraction that deterred him from his purpose—to recover God's presence. The ark had remained out of Jerusalem for about seventy years.[8] Saul hadn't even attempted to recover it during his reign. David, however, desperately wanted God's presence back. To retrieve it, he involved the entire nation. Israel accompanied him with pomp and circumstance—sacrifices, stringed instruments, harps, cymbals, joyous voices, trumpets, worship (see 2 Sam. 6:13–14; 1 Chron. 15:16–24). David didn't dress as royalty but as God's servant and wore an ephod, a priest's garment. He was probably honoring and respecting the Lord with his holy garment for a holy ceremony, plus his actions prophesied about the day we'd be both kings and priests (see Rev. 5:10).

On that trip "David danced before the LORD with all his might" (2 Sam. 6:14), worshiping with abandon like Jehoshaphat's army had done. He was uninhibited by who was around because he was dancing for and praising only One—his Father. The word for "danced" means "spinning around," and was usually performed by women to celebrate success in war.[9] Dancing should be part of praise, warfare, and destiny preparation. David's retrieving God's presence with great humility, reverence, and excitement isn't surprising. He'd seen results of having God in his own life, so he realized what His presence would mean to Israel. He worshipped foolishly and uninhibitedly because he was desperate for God. Worship requires getting over self. Unfortunately, too many don't worship with abandon as David did because it's too undignified. However, those people will paint their faces and get radical, even at t-ball games. Jesus works on our behalf; so He's worthy of radical, foolish praise and worship. After they arrived in Jerusalem, David blessed all Israel with a loaf of bread, a piece of meat, and a raisin cake. After worshiping the Lord, others returned home; then David blessed his house last (see 2 Sam. 6:19–20). Worship fills and enables us to pour into others, plus our own families. Destiny includes blessing others.

MICHAL

David's wife Michal should've led the women who exalted God by dancing alongside her husband during his trek to Jerusalem. Instead, she wasn't even outside like the rest of Israel to welcome him and the ark. She "looked through a window and saw King David leaping and whirling before the Lord; and she despised him in her heart" (2 Sam. 6:16). Her reaction was much different from before when she'd loved and respected him enough to risk her life to help him escape from her father. Perhaps this was a reflection of her dad's apathy toward retrieving the ark. Maybe it showed her lack of love for God because earlier she'd possessed an idol (see 1 Sam. 19:13 NIV). If she still worshipped pagan idols, the ark had little significance for her. Perhaps this scorn was a reflection of pride nurtured in her because of her extravagant lifestyle as a king's daughter and wife. Whatever her reasons, she paid a price for her reaction.

Beware: *Of leaders with idols that stand between them and God.*

Now, as her husband danced back into town with God's presence, her words weren't filled with love for him and God but embarrassment and disdain. She likely shook her finger in his face while she scolded him for making himself a spectacle and wearing the ephod in front of maid servants. She may have called him names as she compared his actions with her dad's dignified comportment. However, David wouldn't let anyone or anything dissuade him from worshiping his Father. He retorted that he was dancing to God who chose him over her dad, and he'd be even more undignified and respected by maid servants. Michal's attitude had consequences. Instead of growing stronger into her destiny as queen, like her husband did as king, she became barren (see 2 Sam. 6:16–23). Lack of intimacy with God brings barrenness, even in our ability to birth destiny.

Beware: *Of those close to you who criticize your worship.*

Araunah's Threshing Floor

Years later, David sinned by numbering Israel. He prayed for God to take away his iniquity. God sent the prophet Gad to give him three choices of punishments: #1. Seven years of famine, #2. Three months of fleeing before his enemies, #3. Three days of plague in the land. David trusted God by leaving punishment to Him. A great plague afflicted Israel; 70,000 died. When David saw an angel by Araunah's threshing floor (Ornan in 1 Chron. 21:15), he and the elders dressed in sackcloth and fell on their faces. He told the Lord he'd brought judgment against others who were innocent and asked Him to afflict only his house (see 2 Sam. 24:10–17). Although this version of the story says this was an angel, later while Solomon was building the temple, Chronicles would say "the Lord had appeared to his father David" (2 Chron. 3:1).

Beware: *Of decisions that negatively affect others.*

Gad instructed David to sacrifice on Araunah's threshing floor. David told Araunah he wanted to buy it, build an altar, and stop the plague. Araunah offered to give the property, plus whatever he needed for sacrificing—oxen, threshing instruments, yokes for wood, and wheat for a grain offering (see 2 Sam. 24:18–22; 1 Chron. 21:18–23). Despite his generous offer, David told Araunah he'd pay full price, saying, "I will surely buy it from you for a price; nor will I offer burnt offerings to the Lord my God with that which costs me nothing" (2 Sam. 24:24). He understood that worship is precious and comes at a price, maybe even lack of decorum or respect of your wife.

Beware: *Of thinking worship has no cost.*

Mary of Bethany learned about worship's cost. As she poured expensive oil of spikenard on Jesus, she sacrificed all—pricey ointment, reputation, others' opinions. Jesus praised her actions (see John 12:3, 7); and He loves our worship, too. Whatever worship costs, we must worship despite that price. We must "present [our] bodies a living sacrifice, holy, acceptable to God, which is [our] reasonable service" (Rom. 12:1). The Greek word used for "service" is *latreia*, meaning "worship."[10] We sacrifice our desires as we give Him worship. This place was Mt. Moriah, which was associated with worship. There, Abraham sacrificed as he took his son over "yonder [to] worship" (Gen. 22:5). This first biblical use of "worship" is *shachah*, meaning "fall down (flat), humbly beseech…, do reverence."[11] Abraham used this time to revere God though He'd asked him to do something incomprehensible. David carried on the family tradition of sacrificing here; and on this mountain, his son built the temple. Circumstances change when we worship at a cost, and the Lord uses it for our destinies. David built the altar and sacrificed a burnt and peace offering, again symbolizing a king and priest. He called on God, who sent fire on the altar and commanded the angel to put down his sword. After David saw that God had answered him, he sacrificed on the threshing floor (see 1 Chron. 21:26–28).

CONCLUSION

From the time he was young and then into his calling, David worshipped the Lord; he even invented instruments of worship (see Amos 6:5). He said to "give unto the Lord the glory due to His name; worship the Lord in the beauty of holiness" (Ps. 29:2). Worship was crucial in David's life and was his lifestyle in both his pre- and post-chosen seasons. His presence should be lovely and necessary as we climb toward destiny.

QUESTIONS TO PONDER
(Answers in Appendix)
THE PHILISTINES

1. Name Israel's leader when the ark was stolen.

2a. What kinds of problems did Philistines experience after stealing it?

2b. How does that apply to our lives?

3. Describe how David escaped potential danger from Achish?

4. When did he feel rejected by Philistines?

5. What was the difference between David's battle plans in the first and second battles with Philistines at Rephaim?

WORSHIP

6. What does the author mean by saying we should make worship a lifestyle?

7. Describe how Jehoshaphat made worship his weapon.

8a. When is the best time to worship?

8b. Give examples of when David worshipped despite sorrow.

9. Tell how all creation worships.

10. What was David's wife's reaction to his returning the ark?

Something to Consider: How do David's enemies/weapon in this chapter speak about our enemies/weapons today?

Chapter Four

GOLIATH

David's Reflections

Let God arise, let His enemies be scattered; let those also who hate Him flee before Him. (Ps. 68:1)

Often enemies seem invincible, but confronting and defeating them will allow God to be glorified beyond measure and us be catapulted toward destiny. Goliath is a well-known character who's been discussed millions of times but appears for one significant event. He was from Gath, a major Philistine city. His name means "passage, revolution, heap."[1] His death was a passage for David, as he became no longer just a shepherd boy who calmed Saul's demons. Through Goliath's defeat, David first showed his mettle and faith. When he left his formidable enemy in a heap, David demonstrated to Israel and their enemies that he was a mighty warrior who trusted God. This story teaches many significant lessons about warfare and destiny journeys.

The Battle Plan

Philistines were encamped in Judah's territory. Soldiers of both armies watched from mountains on each side of a valley. Dressed in battle garb, the groups were ready for war. For forty days, Philistines had offered Israel a challenge which didn't include participation of either nation's entire army. According to Greek warfare rules, a single man per army would fight one battle, with the outcome determining the nation's winner. This person was the "middle man"[2] or "man between two camps,"[3] whose efforts represented the entire army's loss or victory. Goliath was the Philistines' middle man. He stood 9 feet, 9 inches[4] and had superb weapons—a bronze helmet when most soldiers wore leather. His body armor weighed 125 pounds. Bronze armor adorned his legs, and he carried a bronze javelin between his shoulders. His spear's staff was similar to a weaver's beam, the spearhead weighing about seventeen pounds. Preceding him was a shield bearer whose sword wasn't round like Goliath's but longer and larger.[5] With Goliath's size and both men's intimidating armor, Hebrews had been terrorized for more than a month (see 1 Sam. 17:1–11, 16, 21). David's arrival would signal that God's potential is always greater than satan's power.

Beware: *Of reacting in fear when you encounter a formidable enemy.*

The battle had stalled because Israel had named no middle man. Each day, the monstrous Goliath appeared and verbally accosted the Hebrews to answer the challenge to choose an Israeli representative. No one responded, not even the king or his mighty warriors. As a result, the giant taunted Israel, morning and evening. He exhibited scorn as he continued to "defy the armies of Israel" (1 Sam. 17:10). He vowed if he were killed, Philistines would be their servants; if he killed Israel's man, they'd be the Philistines' servants (see 1 Sam. 17:9). Because of his barrage of words and potential for Israel's destruction, King Saul and Israel "were dismayed and greatly afraid" (1 Sam. 17:11). Intimidating enemies make even the most seasoned warriors quake. However, fear can't be part of a successful destiny journey.

Beware: *Of those who taunt and goad you into fear.*

DAVID'S ARRIVAL

Before this Goliath encounter, David had already served in the king's house as Saul's worshipper, but he returned periodically to care for his father's sheep. While in Bethlehem this time, Jesse asked him to take supplies for his three oldest brothers—Eliab, Abinadab, Shammah—who'd followed Saul into battle. After he delivered grain, loaves, and cheese, he could report to his dad about the brothers. Obediently, David rose early the next morning, left the sheep with a keeper, and carried the items his dad had delineated. He had no idea that this day would change his destiny. When he arrived at the camp, the army was preparing and shouting for battle. David dropped off his items with the supply keeper, ran to the troops, and greeted his brothers. As they talked, the giant emerged and bellowed his daily ridicule. At the sight of the colossal man, instead of their recently demonstrated fervor for battle, Israel's men fled and "were dreadfully afraid" (1 Sam. 17:24). Nobody volunteered to be the middle man, though some divulged to David the king's rewards for killing Goliath—money, his daughter's hand in marriage, the victor's father's exemption from taxes. David clarified those incentives (see 1 Sam. 17:13–15, 17–18, 20–27). Then he used Goliath's taunts against him: "who is this uncircumcised Philistine, that he should defy the armies of the living God?" (1 Sam. 17:26, 10).

Beware: *Of those who speak against the Lord.*

David's words angered Eliab. Sometimes those closest may resent our faith and the calling upon our lives. Eliab said David had "pride and insolence of...heart" (1 Sam. 17:28) and accused him of shirking his shepherd duties to come to the battle because of curiosity. David questioned, "What have I done now?" (1 Sam. 17:29). By saying "now," David implied that Eliab's criticism was frequent. His comment about David's responsibility for the sheep was probably an attempt at belittling his brother. He likely still resented Samuel's coming to their house; ignoring him as potential king though he was oldest; then choosing the youngest, a shepherd. His brother's anointing and favor probably made Eliab seethe when he recognized David's potential to fulfill Samuel's prophecy and the favor he'd already gained to live with the current king. That day, the youngest brother showed courage and faith the oldest brother lacked.

Beware: *Of a loved-one's words that could shake your confidence before battle.*

SAUL'S REACTION

Saul sent for David when he heard his comments. David probably hesitated about approaching the king, surrounded by Israel's best warriors. However, while others older and better-trained in warfare demonstrated fear, David didn't falter in his faith. He stated something no Israelite had said for over a month: "Let no man's heart fail because of him; your servant will go and fight with this Philistine" (1 Sam 17:32). The king was likely temporarily relieved that someone was willing to answer the giant's challenge, but he quickly had misgivings. Saul probably already loved David because of their close association, so he feared for David's safety. He also knew someone his age would be an unlikely victor, which would spell doom for David, Saul, and Israel. He declared that David was unable to go because he was young while Goliath had been a man of war from youth (see 1 Sam 17:31–33). When God puts giants in our paths to bring about something great, leadership can shake our confidence and derail God's plan to overcome the daunting enemy.

Beware: *Of those who discount the power of God's anointed.*

David assured Saul he could fight and win. He said he "used to keep his father's sheep" (1 Sam. 17:34); apparently he now worked full time at the palace. He revealed that at least twice he'd protected sheep in dangerous situations—a lion and bear had taken lambs. He pursued, struck, and took back the lambs from the beasts' mouths. When they fought back, he caught the animal by the beard and then hit and killed it. He proclaimed that God, who delivered him from those beasts' paws, would rescue him from the giant's hand. Goliath would be like those animals because he'd defied God's army. David understood covenant and resented that Goliath, who had no covenant with the Lord, dared challenge them. His confidence and authority were contagious, so Saul relented (see 1 Sam. 17:35–37). His allowing David to fight showed understanding of the boy's substance and trust in the Lord. Callings bring enablement and assurance that spill over into others.

UNTESTED WEAPONS

Saul told David to go with God. To help him, he offered his armor: a bronze helmet; and coat of mail (see 1 Sam. 17:37–38), which was a breastplate of metal scales to protect the back and chest.[6] These preeminent Israeli weapons were impressive but likely dwarfed David's young body. After fastening Saul's sword to the armor, "David said to Saul, 'I cannot walk with these, for I have not tested them.' So David took them off" (1 Sam. 17:39). God has given each of us a cache of weapons, and specific ones are needed for different battles during our journeys. A war-time arsenal isn't one-size-fits-all. What works will change from person-to-person and battle-to-battle. If we go to war but haven't regularly employed our armaments, learned their power, or understood how to operate in them, we arrive unprepared to fight against the enemy. If we use them habitually, we're victorious when faced with battle. We must be comfortable with whatever we use. We utilize our weapons regularly so we arrive at life-and-death battles with an arsenal tested through experience.

Beware: *Of thinking elaborate weapons are better.*

How others must've cringed and criticized as David removed Saul's mighty armor. Their feeble optimism likely became powerful pessimism with each piece David peeled off. Then, when he instead took his shepherd's staff and chose stones from the creek, their already-weak hope must've plummeted. David's paltry weapons certainly looked pitiful beside Saul's and Goliath's magnificent arsenals. As Israel's huge adversary roared insults to their army, some probably urged David to put the king's armor back on. Instead, he stored his rocks in a pouch in his shepherd's bag and clutched his sling (see 1 Sam. 17:40). He'd learned how that arsenal worked while protecting his sheep on Bethlehem hills. His shepherd's weapons had been tested often against challenges threatening his flock. He'd learned from experience that often what's needed isn't a king's arsenal but rather a shepherd's, and with testing comes a familiarity that's crucial for battle. Success occurs when we know God's weapons are sure, and those trusted weapons are backed by covenant with Him.

Beware: *Of going into battle with untested weapons.*

The Lord uses what we possess and practice, even a sling and stones. This young shepherd understood the concept of untested armor, and so should we. David wouldn't take Israel's best resources against Goliath without having tested them. Neither should we arrive in battle without advanced knowledge of our armaments. We're told to be "ready in season and out of season" (2 Tim. 4:2). Going into battle isn't when we should decide which weapons are dependable and how to employ them. If we've never used them, we're at a disadvantage. Our weapons should be tested time and again during regular, intimate occasions with our Father. That translates into destiny preparedness.

THE ENEMY'S REACTION

Despite Israel's concern, this boy proceeded confidently with his tested weapon. His approaching Goliath must've created an amusing sight to the giant and massive Philistine army. Guffaws probably erupted in their ranks, but David wasn't deterred. Armed with scant weapons, he drew closer. Simultaneously, Goliath and his shield bearer edged nearer to David. The giant belittled his age and appearance, then acted insulted by the Hebrews' inferior representative. He asked if he were a dog because David was coming with sticks. His booming voice cursed David by his pagan gods and bade him to draw closer so he could feed him to birds and beasts. However, even thunderous threats from that enormous man didn't shake David's confidence in *his* God (see 1 Sam. 17:41–44). He understood what Paul would later say: "God...gives life to the dead and calls those things which do not exist as though they did" (Rom. 4:17). In the natural, he was all-but-dead-and-defeated by this superior creature's hand. However, David was calling things in the Spirit realm into being. He proclaimed triumph; so in God's economy, victory was pronounced into existence. A large chapter in David's destiny story was ready to unfold.

Beware: *Of your reaction to one who threatens or ridicules you.*

David informed Goliath that though he approached with sword, spear, and javelin, David had a greater weapon—the name of his God, whom the giant had defied. God would give David victory and Goliath's head. Israel would defeat the Philistines and give *their* carcasses to birds and beasts (see 1 Sam. 17:45–46). Then, they would know "the Lord does not save with sword and spear; for the battle is the Lord's, and He will give [them] into [Israel's] hand" (1 Sam. 17:47). Too often we undertake the battle ourselves when it belongs to the Lord. Speaking triumph in faith then following God's leading produces His outcome. God would receive glory for this amazing, impossible victory through David's hand because with God, impossibilities become realities (see Matt. 19:26).

Beware: *Of thinking the battle is yours, not God's.*

THE VICTORY

As the giant arose and marched haughtily toward David, the shepherd hastened toward him. Goliath's huge sandals probably raised a swirl of dust as they crunched loudly on the hard, desert ground while he descended to meet his foe. Their booming echo across the mountains likely made the Hebrews, silently watching, even more fearful as he raced down the mountain toward the valley and his mismatched opponent. What a difference between David and other Israelites! Though Eliab and Saul had doubted David's ability, neither they nor any other Hebrew had stepped forward. Instead of running *to* Goliath, they'd run *from* him. To achieve victory, a battle must be engaged. If we flee because an intimidating enemy advances, we can't succeed. In the Lord's name, we run forward in confidence that God will defeat the enemy and use this experience for our promotion. As the opponents approached each other, David reached into his bag and removed one stone (see 1 Sam. 17:48–49). To thrust it, he would've placed the rock into the leather's hollow part that held the cords together. Then, he could gain speed by encircling his head with extended straps. When they were spinning fast enough, he'd let go of one cord so the stone would propel toward Goliath. To be accurate in hitting his target, he would have tested his weapons for many hours on the hillsides.[7]

Beware: *Of warriors who run away from instead of toward the battle.*

David had collected five stones, but he needed just one. The Lord always gives more than we require. He hurled the sling, let the rock soar, and hit Goliath on his forehead. His accuracy was spot on. The stone sank deeply into the giant's head, and he fell on his face onto the ground. With the stone he'd tucked inside his shepherd's bag, he dropped and killed the mighty man. He ran and stood over him (see 1 Sam. 17:49–51). How dynamics had changed from moments earlier when the giant loomed above him! God doesn't see from our vantage point. Observing from His perspective changes things, often in a moment. Oh, what a difference God can make in that instant when we act in faith!

Beware: *Of looking from your viewpoint rather than from God's.*

David had no sword to finish his victory. He slid Goliath's from its sheath and, ironically, cut off the giant's head with his own sword. Disbelieving silence probably permeated both armies as they processed the impossibility of what had just happened. Then, when reality of their champion's death dawned on them, the Philistines didn't submit to Israel as rules of warfare dictated. Instead, they fled. They'd entered that battle with greater weapons, but with an enormous disadvantage. The Philistines had trusted in their hero while David trusted in his God. Men of Judah and Israel rose, shouted, and pursued. Wounded Philistines littered the roads, which proved David's prophetic word about birds eating their carcasses. After Israel's army returned, they plundered Philistine tents. David took the ultimate prize, Goliath's head, to Jerusalem, but he put the armor into his tent (see 1 Sam. 17:51–54). Because David's character was to credit God with victory, not his efforts, the word "tent" probably refers to God's tabernacle.[8] That's consistent with Goliath's sword later being with priests in Nob (see 1 Sam. 21:9).

Beware: *Of thinking your enemy will act with honor after defeat.*

AFTER GOLIATH'S DEATH

Goliath's family didn't forget this defeat. When Philistines and Israel were at war again, David fought and grew faint. Ishbi-Benob, son of a giant, thought he could kill the king with his bronze spear and new sword. Instead, Abishai intervened and killed the giant. Then, war with Philistines again broke out at Gob (in 2 Sam. 21:18; Gezer in 1 Chron. 20:4), and one of David's men killed Saph (Sippai in 1 Chron. 20:4), another giant. In a different war at Gob, Elhanan killed Lahmi, who also had a spear like a weaver's beam. In Goliath's hometown, a giant with six fingers and toes on each hand and foot defied Israel. David's nephew Jonathan killed him. These four giants were killed by David and his servants (see 2 Sam. 21:15–21; 1 Chron. 20:4–7), and apparently were Goliath's brothers. Scripture says "these four were born to the giant" (2 Sam. 21:22). Could the other four stones he picked up from the stream have been for Goliath's brothers? We serve a Lord who knows just what we'll need while we're on our journey then after we arrive.

Beware: *Of residual connections arising after you slay your giant.*

CONCLUSION

We'll encounter daunting enemies as we head toward destiny. David understood that regardless of size, reputation, or superior ability, "they shall fall and perish at Your presence. For [the Lord] maintain[s his] right and…cause;… [He] …destroyed the wicked; [and] blotted out their name forever and ever" (Ps. 9:3–5). The Lord sees who will rise against us and already has a plan for our success, their defeat, and our promotion.

DAVID'S WEAPONS: HOLY SPIRIT

DAVID'S REFLECTIONS

Create in me a clean heart, O God, and renew a steadfast spirit within me. Do not cast me away from Your presence, and do not take Your Holy Spirit from me. Restore to me the joy of Your salvation, and uphold me by Your generous Spirit. (Ps. 51:10–12)

Before He left, Jesus foretold the coming of one of our greatest weapons of warfare: Holy Spirit. When He departed, He said He wouldn't leave us orphans but rather would send Holy Spirit as our Helper. Then He told disciples, "I send the Promise of My Father upon you; but tarry in the city of Jerusalem until you are endued with power from on high" (Luke 24:49). In His resurrected body, Jesus confirmed they'd receive power after Holy Spirit arrived. Jesus' prophecy was fulfilled when Holy Spirit filled the Upper Room with tongues of fire, and people spoke in other tongues. Now, Holy Spirit no longer lives *with* us, but rather *in* us (see Acts 1:8; John 14:17). He's our Source because we're His temple, and His anointing supplies what we need to build that temple. As we journey toward destiny, He's crucial. Before Israel entered the Promised Land, the Lord said He'd never abandon them (see Deut. 31:6). Holy Spirit became our Promised Land experience when He took up abode in us. Because of that, we can be even greater warriors than David.

After that Upper Room event, Peter told Jews that by believing on Jesus, they could receive that "gift of Holy Spirit" (Acts 2:38). Holy Spirit is just that—a gift. With salvation, we receive an infilling of the Trinity—Father, Son, and Holy Spirit. However, more is available than that initial salvation infilling. Some call the next step being "filled with the Spirit" or "baptized" in the Spirit (Eph. 5:18; Acts 1:5) when we choose to activate His gifts with evidence of speaking in tongues. When Holy Spirit comes, He changes everything as He strengthens, empowers, and equips us to know who we are in Christ and to live an overcoming lifestyle. David realized the necessity of God's Spirit as an integral part of his life. The gift of Holy Spirit should be an amazing, vital part of our Christian walk, too.

Before the Upper Room

Before Jesus' ascension and Holy Spirit's arrival in the Upper Room, the Spirit had already been important in lives. He was here since the beginning of time when He hovered over the waters during creation (see Gen. 1:2). Holy Spirit came on judges, too, enabling Othniel to judge Israel and Jephthah to advance toward the Ammonites (see Judg. 3:10; 11:29). He facilitated Gideon's blowing the trumpet to gather warriors and Samson's killing thirty men of Ashkelon and breaking Philistine ropes from his arms (see Judg. 6:34; 14:19; 15:14). Who we are—our gifts and talents—are birthed and nurtured by Holy Spirit (see Exod. 31:2–5). He planted those into us so we could fulfill God's purpose.

In the New Testament while Jesus was on earth, others were directed by Holy Spirit, and one special family was *filled with* the Spirit before the Upper Room. Simeon was led by Holy Spirit to the temple where he saw Baby Jesus. The Spirit descended upon Jesus when He was baptized, and He was filled with Holy Spirit. Before He began His ministry, Holy Spirit led Him to the wilderness for forty days of fasting (see Luke 2:27; 3:21–22; 4:1–2). His cousin, John the Baptist, was filled with the Spirit in utero. At the same time, his mother saw Jesus' mother; John leaped within her; and she, too, was filled with the Spirit. After John's circumcision, his dad also was filled with the Spirit (see Luke 1:15, 41, 67). When John said Jesus would baptize with fire, he understood personally what that power represented (see Matt. 3:11). How awesome for John to be reared in a Spirit-filled family when others had not yet experienced the infilling!

David lived many years before that Upper Room experience, but he was influenced by the Spirit. When he was anointed by Samuel, "the Spirit of the LORD came upon David from that day forward" (see 1 Sam. 16:13). Holy Spirit was so important to him that after he sinned with Bathsheba, David voiced a concern in the above-featured psalm. He pleaded with God not to take His Spirit from him (see Ps. 51:11). Holy Spirit was his powerful weapon as a boy, young man, warrior, and ruler. He was likely in the Spirit's presence while watching sheep, writing worship songs, and protecting his flock. Part of David's last words were about Holy Spirit: "the Spirit of the Lord spoke by me" (2 Sam. 23:2). David's stories show how he and others depended upon Holy Spirit's empowerment to take them into the fullness of their destinies.

THE GIFTS

After we're filled with the Spirit, His gifts are activated to help us by His power. They're divided into three categories. Revelation gifts are words of knowledge, words of wisdom, and discernment of spirits. Speaking gifts are prophecy, different kinds of tongues, and interpretation of tongues. Power gifts are faith, gifts of healings, and working of miracles (see 1 Cor. 12:8–10). I've operated in all these gifts since I was young and often have seen the enemy's plans dissipate. One Sunday morning during the sermon at church, I saw a clear vision, a word of wisdom. I was sitting beside my three-year-old granddaughter's hospital bed. We live twelve hours away, so I knew her injury would be serious if I were with her. I prayed intensely during the service. Then, as we left church, I called my daughter and told her to anoint our little girl. Before the day was over, she'd climbed on the kitchen island and gotten too close to the edge. My daughter caught her as she plummeted over the side. We rejoiced that, once again, God had revealed and protected. Then, two days later, she went to her room to get a toy. She was there about a minute when my daughter heard a crash. My granddaughter had scaled open drawers, and her dresser had fallen forward. Instead of being caught under that heavy furniture, her daughter was standing across the room by the bed. My granddaughter later told me that as the dresser fell forward, someone (an angel) picked her up and set her by the bed. Both times the Lord negated satan's plans for our precious baby's harm, and He even sent a heavenly emissary to accomplish that. Each occasion when we war with the gifts, God responds with mighty victories.

THE ARMOR

Besides His gifts, Holy Spirit provides a heavenly arsenal for success in battle. Each day we should suit up in the entire armor to protect us all around from the enemy. Defensive weapons are the belt of truth, breastplate of righteousness, gospel of peace on our feet, shield of faith, and helmet of salvation (see Eph. 6:11, 14–17). The final weapon is our offensive one—the "sword of the Spirit, which is the word of God" (Eph. 6:17). God's written Word is crucial in battle. I'll discuss that in my chapter, "God's Word and

Trust." However, this use of "word" isn't expressing the Scripture's necessity as a weapon of warfare. Here, our armor's "word" is *rhema*, a Holy Spirit *now* "utterance,"[1] that allows us to navigate through situations the enemy hurls.

A *rhema* is God's powerful word going forth to accomplish what's needed for that time. It may be revealed in many ways—TV, the Bible, a dream, a casual comment from a friend, etcetera. The *rhema* may include a prophetic action to achieve victory—dip seven times in the river, march around the wall in silence for a specific number of days and times before sounding the trumpet, or stretch your rod over the sea (see 2 Kings 5:10; Josh. 6:16; Exod. 14:26). God's *rhema* provides exactly the weapon and battle plan needed for today's skirmish. Whether to go or stay, march or stand, a *rhema* becomes our victory strategy. Each battle requires a new plan to defeat the enemy, who already knows yesterday's tactics. Moses said that although God doesn't reveal everything to people, when He does, those revelations belong to us and future generations (see Deut. 29:29). That's how a *rhema* works. Once God gives it, it's ours!

Instructing David to march with a sound in the mulberry trees was a prophetic action, God's method of operation to bring victory over the Philistines. We've witnessed the Lord delivering people many times by obeying these sometimes-silly, prophetic actions. I once spoke at a church where the pastor had suffered a stroke. In the two years since the event, he'd struggled with residual effects. That night as we ministered at the altar, the Lord told me to do a prophetic action. I was to walk five times around him as if I were wrapping him in a gauze bandage. With each circle, both he and I felt an anointing so strongly we could hardly stand. By the fifth time, power was tangible. At the end of the service, he testified. He hadn't been able to move his toes, and now he could. His mobility had improved in other ways, too. As ridiculous as that scenario would be to men, God's foolishness and weakness are wiser and stronger than whatever man concocts (see 1 Cor. 1:25). That laughable, prophetic action accomplished what doctors couldn't.

After listing armor pieces, Paul adds one more instruction: "praying always with all prayer and supplication in the Spirit" (Eph. 6:18). Prayer language is part of the gift of tongues, and the armor is activated by praying in the Spirit. Holy Spirit's language is a powerful, enemy-defeating weapon most Christians ignore because they misunderstand or have heard faulty teaching. The enemy doesn't comprehend prayer language and therefore can't formulate a battle plan against it. That language reveals God's wisdom, builds faith, and allows us to pray effectively when we don't know how (see 1 Cor. 2:6; Jude 20; Rom. 8:26). Something's bothering you, but you don't know what. Holy Spirit does. Your teenager is acting strangely, but you have no idea what's happening. Holy Spirit does. Something's wrong in your body, but doctors can't diagnose the problem. Holy Spirit knows. How can prayers be ineffective if Holy Spirit is praying to the Father in His language? Tongues are an amazing, enemy-defeating weapon.

DAVID'S STORY

Holy Spirit's gifts allow us to fulfill our destinies effectively. The gifts separate us from others because Holy Spirit reveals situations then proves Himself. For example, Daniel's life was spared, and he was promoted because of his gift of dream interpretation (see Dan. 2:48). I wonder if Solomon thought about his dad's gifts when he penned, "A man's gift makes room for him, and brings him before great men" (Prov. 18:16). David entrusted battles to Holy Spirit and used His weapons and gifts many times. Through Holy Spirit's ability, David's harp became an instrument of deliverance as He was brought before the king to battle evil spirits. When God told David the men of Keilah would betray him to Saul, David knew to flee from certain capture and death. As he sought God's direction, twice Holy Spirit gave him words of wisdom about his army's deployment in the Valley of Rephaim—to go before them to strike the Philistines' camp then advance quickly when he heard the sound of their marching. By doing this, David had great victories (see 1 Sam. 16:23; 23:12–13; 2 Sam. 5:19–25).

David's experience with Goliath showed his use of the gifts. He received a revelation about how to achieve victory, the method of operation: One stone and a sling would do the job. He told Goliath that God would give him the giant's head, and birds would eat the Philistines' bodies. Those prophecies came to pass. That revelation was a word of wisdom and prophecy, but it also demonstrated the gift of faith when God planted supernatural assurance of victory into David (see 1 Sam. 17:40, 46). Goliath was defeated because David had total confidence in God to triumph through simple weapons.

When David's life was directed by Holy Spirit, He prevailed and made great leaps toward his ultimate destiny.

The gift of prophecy operated through David besides when he told Goliath of their impending victory. As he set up his tabernacle, he appointed people "who should prophesy with harps, stringed instruments, and cymbals" (1 Chron. 25:1). His prophetic word about Jesus was referenced by Luke: "Scripture [was] fulfilled, which the Holy Spirit spoke before by the mouth of David concerning Judas" (Acts 1:16). David wielded the gift of discernment of spirits as he played the harp when demons oppressed Saul. Other times, Holy Spirit's direction affected his life. Nathan received a word of knowledge about David's sexual sin, and his confrontation with the king allowed David to repent (see 2 Sam. 12:7). All of these prepared him for intense warfare his God-given purpose required.

Holy Spirit is that "still small voice" Elijah heard on the mountain (1 Kings 19:12). That gentle voice spoke to Samuel, well-respected as a prophet from his youth. Even before they met, Saul's opinion of Samuel's prophetic ability was that whatever Samuel said came to pass. Later, he'd give Saul a word of knowledge that the missing donkeys were found. God's final word about Saul while Samuel was alive would say God was removing his anointing. Samuel also told David through a word of wisdom that he'd someday be king, and Holy Spirit gave him a word of knowledge that Saul had disobeyed. Before God revealed Israel's first king, "the Lord had told Samuel in his ear" that His choice would come the next day (see 1 Sam. 9:15). Then, as Samuel observed Saul, God confirmed (see 1 Sam. 9:6, 20; 15:28; 16:12; 9:17). Holy Spirit dealt with David after he numbered Israel, and his "heart condemned him" (2 Sam. 24:10). Whispering in our ear is Holy Spirit's job—an unction. He becomes our "light that shines in a dark place" (2 Pet. 1:19). Never have I asked Holy Spirit to light my path that He has failed to do so, whether for something big like major decisions or simple like finding a lost item.

PROPHETIC INTEGRITY

Using our gifts requires uprightness, and Saul shows how lack of integrity negatively affects their operation. Before Samuel anointed Saul as king, he gave Saul a prophetic word that as he traveled to Tabor, he'd meet three men with three young goats, three loaves of bread, and a skin of wine. Then he'd go by a hill with a Philistine garrison and meet prophets in the city where all would prophesy. That happened just as he said (see 1 Sam. 10:3–5; 9). Prophets descended from a high place with stringed instruments, tambourines, flutes, and harps. During all this, Saul prophesied as Samuel said: "the Spirit of the Lord will come upon you, and you will prophesy with them and be turned into another man" (see 1 Sam. 10:6). When this occurred, others noticed Saul's prophetic words and asked, "Is Saul also among the prophets?" (1 Sam. 10:11). At this time, he was genuine. However, later people would question his prophetic legitimacy.

Beware: *Of leaders who don't operate in Holy Spirit.*

When Holy Spirit came upon Saul, he was indeed turned into a different man. After he heard the Ammonites' demand to put out the Israelites' eyes, Holy Spirit again came upon him, and he became angry. This demand inspired him to attack and prevail while cementing his kingship. A while before, he was so timid that he'd hidden. With Holy Spirit he was able to lead God's great nation (see 1 Sam. 11:6, 11). Later, Saul's character plummeted after he heard Israel's praise of David. He became "very angry, and the saying displeased him…. So Saul eyed David from that day forward" (1 Sam. 18:8–9). In other words, for the rest of his life, Saul scrutinized David with unforgiveness and suspicion.[2] When a distressing spirit overcame him, Saul "prophesied inside the house" (1 Sam. 18:10). This Hebrew word for "prophesied" is *naba*, the same word used for genuine examples of prophecy. However, one definition of this word is to "make self a prophet."[3]

Beware: *Of those whose actions bring a black mark on the prophetic.*

This scenario happens too often when people erroneously position themselves as God's mouth-pieces when it's all about self. Ezekiel says, "woe to the foolish prophets, who follow their own spirit and have seen nothing!" (Ezek. 13:3). Sometimes their falseness isn't malicious, but it's *self* when they add up their conclusions and present them as prophecy. Saul's attitude and actions belied prophetic character. When the evil spirit arose, David played to calm it, but Saul had much evil in his heart. When he tried twice to kill David, Saul also *prophesied.* How can *prophets* speak God's heart of love when they're under demonic influence? When their heart is filled with evil—jealousy, displeasure, hatred, fear, anger, suspicion, and unforgiveness (see 1 Sam. 18:8–12)? How can the prophetic ring true when that person has murder in his or her heart and actively tries to make it happen—murder of another's reputation, relationships, peace of mind?

Jesus alluded to character when He said many would operate in Holy Spirit's gifts and call Him Lord, but He wouldn't recognize them because they "practice lawlessness" (see Matt. 7:22–23). Some versions translate "lawlessness" as "iniquity" (KJV). Jesus asked Pharisees, "how can you, being evil, speak good things?" (Matt. 12:34). Bitter water mixed with sweet becomes tainted (see James 3:11), and so is prophecy that comes forth. Saul prophesied from a lawless heart filled with ugly things. That's not God's heart.

Beware: *Of prophecy from those whose hearts are filled with evil toward others.*

Saul again demonstrated faulty prophecy after David fled to Samuel and told him what Saul had done. When Saul was told where David was hiding, he sent messengers to capture him. As genuine prophets led by Samuel prophesied, Holy Spirit came on Saul's messengers also to prophesy. Saul sent emissaries two more times with the same results. Finally, he went personally to take care of the David problem. The Spirit of God came on him, he stripped off his clothes, and he prophesied before Samuel. He lay naked all day and night. This seems symbolic of his kingship and prophetic anointing he wore no longer. People again asked if Saul were among the prophets but this time sarcastically or unbelievingly, having seen his faulty character (see 1 Sam. 19:19–24). Saul's actions against David and the prophetic were inexcusable. He'd been chosen, and "to whom much is given, from him much will be required" (Luke 12:48). Many forget that when they operate with little integrity while using their gifts or interacting with others. Holy Spirit is an amazing weapon to fulfill our destinies, but operating in His gifts is a privilege that requires responsibility.

Beware: *Of those who don't treat their gifts with respect.*

CONCLUSION

Holy Spirit is crucial for our walk. Recently a friend who'd just been filled with the Spirit told me she felt like she'd been living in a black and white world when Technicolor was available. Jesus is the door (see John 10:7) for Holy Spirit to enter, but more is available after He comes in. When you open that door, life in Holy Spirit unlocks a new, colorful world. David said, "Where can I go from Your Spirit? Or where can I flee from Your presence? If I ascend into heaven, You are there; if I make my bed in hell, behold, You are there" (Ps. 139:/–8). Holy Spirit is a powerful necessity in our destiny walks.

QUESTIONS TO PONDER
(Answers in Appendix)
GOLIATH

1. Explain the term *middle man*.

2. How did David's and others' responses to Goliath's taunts differ?

3. Explain tested versus untested weapons.

4. Describe Goliath's reaction to David.

5. Contrast responses of the two armies after Goliath was defeated.

HOLY SPIRIT

6. What's the difference in how Holy Spirit related to people in the Old and New Testaments?

7. Explain what being "filled with the Spirit" means.

8. List Holy Spirit's gifts in their categories.

9. What are items in the Ephesians 6 armor?

10. Give examples of how David used the gifts and identify them.

11. How did Saul demonstrate false prophecy?

Something to Consider: How does David's enemy/weapon in this chapter speak about our enemies/weapons today?

Chapter Five

SHIMEI

DAVID'S REFLECTIONS

Hide me from the secret plots of the wicked, from the rebellion of the workers of iniquity, who sharpen their tongue like a sword, and bend their bows to shoot their arrows—bitter words, that they may shoot in secret at the blameless. (Ps. 64:2–4)

Some enemies despise us because of our anointing, and they accost us at our worst times. Too many are self-focused—their lives, families, destinies, promotions. Because of this, they become enemies of our destinies and are determined to destroy our reputations, positions, and callings. Shimei, who caused David and Solomon grief, appeared briefly during David's life when he created a confrontation. Part of his name's meaning is "my reputation; my fame."[1] This name suits his character. He didn't want the Lord's will but was consumed with himself and how David's kingship negatively affected him. He was Saul's relative, so he felt David had stolen the kingdom from the house of Benjamin. During a difficult time for David, Shimei bombarded him with curses, criticism, assaults, accusations, insults, pride, and envy.

Beware: *Of those who care more about self-promotion than God's choice of whom He'll use.*

SHIMEI'S ATTACKS

David's beloved son Absalom had betrayed him, so he fled from Jerusalem. However, as is often true during hardest trials, more attacks occurred. In Bahurim, he passed the house of Shimei, who shouted insults. He tormented David both by swearing and "cursing continuously" (2 Sam. 16:5). That phrase means "asking God to destroy David."[2] This tactic typifies those who *pray* curses on others while sanctimoniously acting as if they're voicing the Lord's will. Shimei's comments may have been alluding to the curse against David's house because of his sin against Uriah (see 2 Sam. 12:10). However, even if that were the case, his railing was wrong. David once said an upright person doesn't, "backbite with his tongue, nor does evil to his neighbor, nor does he take up a reproach against his friend" (Ps. 15:3). Shimei's actions were opposite of that.

Beware: *Of those who "pray" curses against others.*

I envision Shimei with a perpetual scowl as he confronted the king. He'd probably despised David ever since he'd heard of David's calling while Saul was still king. When we hold onto bitterness, it changes us. Even our appearance. Even our destinies. Shimei's vicious attacks showed how his hatred became a cancer that ate at him and caused him to defame God's anointed. He called David "bloodthirsty" and "rogue" (2 Sam. 16:7) and said that he'd brought blood on Saul's house (see 2 Sam. 16:8). Ironically, not too long after this, God would say Israel's famine was "because of Saul and his bloodthirsty house" (2 Sam. 21:1). Since he was of the house of Benjamin, Shimei was included in that. The enemy behaves this way—accusing others of something for which he's guilty. Perhaps Shimei was referencing David's living with the Philistines before the battle that had taken Saul's and his sons' lives. The implication was that David had contributed to that tragedy. Perhaps he felt David had been responsible for Ishbosheth's and Abner's murders after David had negotiated for the throne. Maybe Shimei knew what the Lord would later speak about David not building the temple because of bloodshed (see 2 Sam. 3:12; 1 Chron. 22:8). Whatever the reference, David likely comprehended all those meanings and was hurt by each.

Beware: *Of those who harbor resentment about your calling.*

I wonder if David thought of Shimei when he wrote, "let the lying lips be put to silence, which speak insolent things proudly and contemptuously against the righteous" (Ps. 31:18). Shimei said God had delivered his kingdom into Absalom's hand because of David's killing Saul and his house, then reigning in Saul's place (see 2 Sam. 16:8). This shows how one with a self-centered nature attacks the anointing with lies or twisted accusations. Many enemy attacks are hurtful, false words that are truth's opposite. David hadn't killed Saul's family, but the enemy spouts enough truth to make a lie believable. Satan's a liar, and half-truths that seem believable are still lies. How Shimei's false words must've stung David. He'd loved Saul and Jonathan and mourned their passing. David and Jonathan's souls were knit together. Even after his friend's death, he honored their covenant when he realized Jonathan's son was alive. He'd never been disloyal to Saul and returned good for Saul's evil. David said people like Shimei, "sharpen their tongues like a serpent; the poison of asps is under their lips" (Ps. 140:3).

Beware: *Of those who take advantage of your lowest point to hurl unwarranted accusations.*

The psalmist's comment describes Shimei perfectly: "My enemies reproach me all day long; those who deride me swear an oath against me" (Ps. 102:8). Shimei continually followed David along the hillside, while cursing, throwing stones at him and his servants, and kicking up dust (see 2 Sam. 16:13). The king must have been especially hurt when Shimei threw rocks at him. That act was significant. This was similar to someone pitching stones at an annoying animal. Also, Israel surely still talked about the giant's defeat with a single stone, and the irony of stones being hurled at their great victor certainly didn't escape David. In addition, stoning was a popular way to kill those who deserved punishment. This showed Shimei's state of mind.

Beware: *Of those who throw stones of hatred and kick up dirt at you.*

GOD'S WILL

Abishai was David's nephew, a great warrior and loyal to David. However, his character leaned toward killing. He wanted to kill Saul when opportunities arose. He'd been complicit in killing Abner. At one time, he'd killed 300 with his sword (see 1 Sam. 26:8; 2 Sam. 3:30; 23:18). Now, this man of war was incensed by Shimei's actions and jumped to David's defense, saying, "why should this dead dog curse my lord the king? Please let me go over and take off his head!" (2 Sam. 16:9). David trusted God so much that during trials he gave his fate to Him. He refused Abishai's offer because Shimei's cursing may have been the Lord's will. He said if his own son sought his demise, why not Shimei, who was in Saul's lineage? A Benjamite's curse seemed small by comparison, especially if it were God's will (see 2 Sam. 16:10–11). We're His chosen, but God often allows events to happen for a greater purpose. If He's called and anointed us, we can be sure everything that happens in our lives will work for our good (see Rom. 8:28). Even bad things. Knowing this, we can weather life's storms with peace.

Beware: *Of trying to settle disputes through your strength.*

David made another declaration about trials: "It may be that the Lord will look on my affliction, and…repay me with good for [Shimei's] cursing this day" (2 Sam. 16:12). When others bombard us with unfair words or actions, that attack may be a tool God will use for blessing and promotion. I experienced this firsthand. I once was confronted by someone to whom I'd been kind, despite her repeatedly talking badly about me. Then she became more vicious. She and her friends behaved like Shimei—throwing stones, hurling accusations, kicking up dirt. They even spoke curses over me and "prayed" for my destruction. Like Shimei and David, their lies and half-truths followed me. Does that resemble persecutions against you and your anointing—lies and character assassinations with the end goal of breaking you?

Initially, I was consumed and devastated by the same dynamics that occurred between David and Shimei. However, this type of attack comes from satan's arsenal. His character is reflected in his name's meanings: "contrary; adversary; enemy."[3] Though people aren't the enemy, he uses them to reproach the innocent rather than reveal evil residing in the one through whom he's actually operating. Unfortunately, those people are so deceived they often believe they've done nothing wrong. Jesus said that at times, like Shimei's attack, someone could even kill you and think he or she is doing God's work (see John 16:2). The devil's nature is lies, and "there is no truth in him" (John 8:44). He's a "thief [who] does not come except to steal, and to kill, and to destroy" (John 10:10). The NIV version uses the word "only." The enemy has only one purpose—to wreak havoc. And he does his job very well. He wants to steal from us—our peace, reputation, testimony. If that doesn't work, he tries to kill and destroy us. He'd like to take us out prematurely so we *never* fulfill our destiny and its kingdom consequences. However, this scripture also says that while the enemy brings death, Jesus brings abundant life. God's good all the time, but the devil is bad all the time. No matter the attack, peace and victory come as we trust Him to protect us and the work He's started in us.

Beware: *Of those who accuse others to shift blame from themselves.*

Many who hurl accusations and dirt are behaving in the Shimei spirit. We have a choice of how to react—lose sleep by fretting like I did, become defensive and try to justify ourselves, or go after them for revenge. Those are flesh choices, and flesh drives sin; if we live in the flesh, we don't please God (see Rom. 7:18; 8:8). Often, our worst enemy is our flesh. On the other hand, wisdom is understanding God's will and being filled with works of the Spirit, not the flesh (see Eph. 5:17–18). The "Spirit...gives life; the flesh profits nothing" (John 6:63). The Spirit produces life while bringing death to sin. If we dwell in the Spirit rather than the flesh, Holy Spirit perfects us, not the flesh (see Gal. 3:3).

Beware: *Of desiring what the flesh wants, not the Spirit.*

When my situation seemed the worst, during another sleepless "flesh" night, Holy Spirit spoke to me the same thing David declared to Abishai—"Promotion's coming." I took Him at His word and rejoiced instead of grieving. These Shimei attacks didn't break me, especially after God's promise. Although the next few weeks and months were still filled with others' stones and dirt following me, I trusted Him and eventually stopped allowing it to bother me. Promotion was coming. Within months, God's word came to pass, and breakthrough happened in many areas of our lives. We're not to fear the enemy's threats (see 1 Pet. 3:14). David didn't fear or allow assaults to derail him because he, too, knew promotion was coming. As a matter of fact, he and his weary people didn't run from Shimei, but they rested there (see 2 Sam. 16.14). That shows me several things. Others' attacks are draining, so we need to refresh ourselves with the Word, worship, prayer, sleep. David trusted God, so he could rest even during the storm. We don't have to escape those who persecute us but can stay right where the enemy lives because we're covered.

AFTER ABSALOM'S DEFEAT

After conquering an enemy, a good leader understands that vengeance isn't the goal against those who opposed him or her. David and Shimei met again after David prevailed over Absalom. He started back to Jerusalem, so Judah went to escort him across the Jordan. Shimei arrived with a large group to meet David: 1,000 men of Benjamin; Ziba; fifteen of his sons; and twenty servants. They preceded him as a ferry carried David and his household back home. When he crossed, Shimei fell before him and begged the king not to hold him accountable for his actions. Many enemies vocally oppose us during hard times; when we're restored, they're like Shimei—a sycophant, groveling before us to regain favor. These opportunists are about self, so others' callings don't matter except for how they affect them. Shimei acknowledged his sin but endeavored to mitigate it by saying David should consider his being the first of Israel to meet the king after the insurrection. Abishai, still angry about the treatment of David, wanted to kill him because cursing God's anointed deserved death. David said Shimei nor anyone else would be put to death in Israel that day. A good leader can forgo revenge because forgiveness is more powerful than a sword (see 2 Sam. 19:16–23). David swore not to kill Shimei then, but he didn't trust him either. Sometimes, when evil arises, that attitude infects others, so we should cut off its head immediately like Abishai wanted to do. Sometimes, though, God has us wait for a season.

Beware: *Of those who so adamantly opposed you yet suddenly show support.*

David honored his oath not to kill Shimei; but as he neared death, he gave Solomon instructions regarding him. He reminded his son of Shimei's actions. He said he vowed not to kill him with the sword, but consequences still should occur. He told Solomon to hold him responsible for his actions but left the punishment to Solomon's discretion (see 1 Kings 2:8). David knew his son understood what he "ought to do... [to] bring [Shimei's] gray hair down to the grave with blood" (1 Kings 2:9). David may have given these instructions for revenge. However, more likely he understood that one with such evil character could negatively influence Solomon's reign. David knew Shimei would eventually give Solomon a reason to kill him, and he did.

Beware: Of thinking God's delay means no consequences will come for attacking God's anointed.

After David died, Solomon called for Shimei. He didn't kill him but told him to build a house and remain in Jerusalem. If he ever crossed the Brook Kidron, he'd be killed. Shimei praised and accepted this arrangement and vowed to do as Solomon commanded. He did stay for three years. Then two of his slaves ran away to Gath, and Shimei retrieved them. When Solomon heard he'd left Jerusalem then returned, he confronted Shimei about the disregard for the king's command and his own oath. He said Shimei had proven "all the wickedness [he] did to...David; therefore the Lord [would] return [his] wickedness on [his] own head" (1 Kings 2:44). Solomon commanded Benaiah to kill Shimei (see 1 Kings 2:36–46).

Beware: Of those with weak character who will go back on their word for selfish motives.

CONCLUSION

Our destiny journeys include enemies who want to destroy us for many reasons. If we react as David did, we can say, "Make haste to help me, O Lord! Let them be ashamed and confounded who seek my life; let them be turned back and confused who desire my hurt" (Ps. 70:1–2). If we trust the Lord during trials, we're one step closer to fulfilling our divine destinies and trusting His wisdom for attacks that plague us once we've arrived at our purpose.

DAVID'S WEAPONS: THE ANOINTING

DAVID'S REFLECTIONS

Now I know that the LORD saves His anointed; He will answer him from His holy heaven with the saving strength of His right hand. (Ps. 20:6)

Victory in warfare is assured when we operate in the anointing. Every Christian has a purpose: to "go into the world and preach the gospel" (Mark 16:15). Beyond that is our individual calling. I once heard a preacher say God's call is like a birthmark. You didn't ask for it, and you can't wash it off. However, being called doesn't mean we automatically attain destiny fulfillment; on the contrary, "many are called, but few are chosen" (Matt. 22:14). Being called is *kletos*, meaning to be "invited."[1] Then, after the calling comes the equipping to get ready to be chosen. The word "chosen" is *eklektos*, meaning "select; by impli. favorite."[2] What we do with our calling in preparation for its fulfillment determines whether we move from being invited to selected. Paul said he operated in discipline to bring his body under subjection lest by his actions he "should become disqualified" (1 Cor. 9:27). God has a plan, but our responsibility is to keep our qualification.

Many missions exist and a multitude of ways to do them. Before Samuel declared Saul's kingship, he asked Saul to eat and said to "set...apart" a portion for Saul (1 Sam. 9:23). God calls us for destinies He's set aside for us. We're set apart, and no one's calling is like ours. For that calling, He considers many aspects: interests, intellect, experiences, talents, gifts, strengths, weaknesses, personalities. God won't put us into a destiny we're unable to do. He has plans, "an expected end" (Jer. 29:11 KJV), and His design is much better than our expectations. However, once we're called for His purpose, much must occur before we become chosen. He grooms us as we travel toward destiny. When we're summoned, responding is up to us.

Before we pursue our callings, we should assess *if* we want to step into the calling and *why* we want it. Some aspire to work for God to have wealth, recognition, or other self-serving motivations. However, our passions should be to please God and serve Him and others. David demonstrated that the

Connie Hunter-Urban

journey toward God's plan isn't the easy choice. Because of this concept, Jesus told multitudes that before they start toward the promise, they should "count the cost" (Luke 14:28). After Paul's Damascus Road experience, Ananias told Saul "how many things he [would] suffer" for Jesus (Acts 9:16). Despite this warning, Saul, who became Paul, chose the calling. He used the metaphor of our calling as a race. Once we accept, we should run this race like it's a cherished prize (see 1 Cor. 9:24). Often our journey seems far away from the prize. Only with our spiritual eye can we see the goal when everything looks unreachable.

WHOM GOD CHOOSES

God doesn't always choose the best that man has to offer. He takes the ordinary then makes the extraordinary. Moses was chosen despite a speech impediment. Jeremiah was picked although he was young (see Exod. 4:10; Jer. 1:6–7). Mary of Bethany had a bad reputation and was criticized as a poor choice to anoint Jesus. At one time Mary Magdalene was demon-possessed and probably a harlot (see Luke 7:39; Mark 16:9). When Gideon was visited to receive his calling, the Angel of the LORD proclaimed him a "mighty man of valor!" though he feared the Midianites and hid his produce from them (see Judg. 6:11–12). When Amos was criticized for his prophecies, he responded that he wasn't a trained "prophet, nor...son of a prophet, but...a sheepbreeder and a tender of sycamore fruit" (Amos 7:14). Jesus didn't pick disciples based on status. They were in large part fishermen. Peter and John were described as "uneducated and untrained" (Acts 4:13), yet they influenced people then and now. King Saul was from the tribe of Benjamin, the smallest of all tribes, and his family was the least of Benjamin (see 1 Sam. 9:21). Despite qualifications, Saul and David were God's choices to lead Israel. God sees who we'll become, not past or current circumstances or earthly status. With man, we may be the last picked because what's "last will be first, and the first last" (Matt. 20:16). God chooses based on *His* criteria, and often that's regular people like us.

Beware: *Of those who think they know whom God should choose.*

David understood that no matter if others see our potential, God does. He said we're "fearfully and wonderfully made" and that God's "eyes saw [our] substance, being yet unformed. And in [His] book they all were written, the days fashioned for [him], when as yet there were none of them" (Ps. 139:14, 16). Before we existed, He knew us, planned our destinies, and wrote about us in His book. He saw potential even while we were making mistakes. He chooses the weak or foolish things "to put to shame the things which are mighty" (1 Cor. 1:27). Paul should know. He wasn't a great choice because of his past persecution of Christians, but he ended up writing a majority of New Testament books. Sometimes God selects us women, someone with a shady past, those shunned by others, simple fishermen, or not seminary-educated people. No matter whom God selects, His choice isn't about our ability but about His through us. His ability, our availability.

Beware: *Of feeling unworthy to be chosen.*

ANOINTING

Once God highlights our calling, much must occur as we "press toward the goal for the prize of the upward call of God in Christ Jesus" (Phil. 3:14). Callings and anointings go hand-in-hand. No one can consummately do his or her calling without Holy Spirit empowerment. That word *anointing* is often misunderstood. One practice in Christian churches is to put oil on someone and pray (see James 5:14). Another meaning, though, is enablement by Holy Spirit to do a specific act. Holy Spirit's anointing empowers us to do what we could not otherwise—step into the fullness of our calling, bring healing to another, write a powerful song, preach a word that draws the lost, rule God's nation as its greatest king.

This passage from my book, *Be Healed!* describes the anointing:

> The anointing is Holy Spirit's ability that comes upon you
> to enable you to do many things…. He plants His ability to
> accomplish what He wants, when He wants. I think of the
> anointing like adrenaline. You have it in you all the time,
> but when a dire need arises—a child is trapped beneath a

car—it escalates to allow you to perform feats you couldn't ordinarily do.[3]

I've witnessed this concept many times. One night as our pastor made his way down a prayer line, his intense anointing preceded him. As he drew toward me, that anointing grew progressively stronger. I couldn't stay upright by the time he reached me. As I lay there slain in the Spirit, the Lord did a mighty work in me. Many received much that night because the anointing empowered Pastor to impart to others.

DAVID'S ANOINTING

While Samuel still mourned Saul's being stripped of his kingdom, God told him to fill his horn with oil and go to Jesse the farmer's house in Bethlehem. He was to anoint one of his sons as the next king. This anointing would literally be with oil, but it would also represent a spiritual-destiny anointing. When he arrived, Jesse and his sons gathered around. He sanctified them then asked to sacrifice. Samuel used this opportunity to observe the sons and ascertain whom to anoint. He eyed Eliab, the oldest, and thought certainly he would be the Lord's choice. God told him, "Do not look at his appearance or at his physical stature, because I have refused him. For the Lord does not see as man sees; for man looks at the outward appearance, but the Lord looks at the heart" (1 Sam. 16:7). What a lesson—don't always trust our opinions! As Samuel studied Jesse's impressive sons, God told him His choice wasn't any who stood there. He was puzzled until he asked if Jesse had others. Jesse belittled David by saying, "There remains yet the youngest, and there he is, keeping the sheep" (1 Sam. 16:11). "Yet the youngest!" Of all people, David's brothers and dad should've known his substance and potential. Instead, they'd neither brought him inside nor included him as one of Jesse's sons (see 1 Sam. 16:1, 5–6, 8, 11).

When Jesse told Samuel about David, he said to, "Send and bring him; for we will not sit down till he comes here" (1 Sam. 16:11). Having his older brothers, dad, and this great prophet stand until David entered showed God had significant plans for that insignificant boy. David wasn't the best choice—he was the youngest and worked with sheep. He was probably illegitimate (see Ps. 51:5). He was later disrespected by his brother Eliab (see 1 Sam. 17:28), proving what the Lord told Samuel about Eliab's outward appearance versus the heart. Sadly, the dynamics of loved ones' lack of support and belief for our anointing comes as part of our calling, even with Jesus (see John 7:5). Despite family dynamics, "David went on and became great, and the Lord of hosts was with him" (1 Chron. 11:9). Anointing is key to where God will take us and what He'll do for and through us.

Beware: *Of feeling discouraged when others don't recognize your substance.*

David entered. He was young and had a ruddy complexion, bright eyes, and good looks. When God said he was the one, the brothers probably glanced at each other in disbelief and resentment. Surely God had made a mistake, but the prophet continued to address David. Samuel anointed David with oil in the midst of his brothers. Holy Spirit then settled on David that day and changed his life. When Holy Spirit engulfed Mary and impregnated her, her destiny was also established (see 1 Sam. 16:12–13; Luke 1:35). After God's Spirit comes upon us, He implants His destiny seed inside, and our lives will never be the same. This would be the first of three times David would be anointed as king, and this first anointing provided Holy Spirit as a powerful tool for David to fulfill future anointings. The second time, he'd be anointed king over Judah. Seven years later, he'd again be anointed—as king of all Israel (see 2 Sam. 2:4; 5:3). In the meantime Saul was king, and David had much to do to prepare for his royal destiny.

Beware: *Of leaders who operate without Holy Spirit or the anointing.*

FAVOR

Favor works in tandem with the anointing. The anointing or lack of can change our kingship. Before God's anointing departed from Saul, he did mighty works. After it departed, he became so desperate to hear from God that he consulted a medium for a séance with Samuel. David's anointing, on the other hand, brought favor with God and others. By himself, he was ill-equipped to be a warrior and defeat powerful enemies; with Holy Spirit's anointing, opponents fell. Lions and bears relinquished stolen sheep.

He killed those predators then the giant who plagued Israel's flock. Our anointing is to be used for others. By making ourselves a servant, we gain much that moves us toward destiny. That's favor.

While a career focuses on upward mobility, a calling often takes us downward as a servant. Nehemiah, Joshua, and Elisha all stepped into God's plan after their seasons of servitude. Though David was anointed as king, he first entered the palace as a servant. Saul's servants recognized his anointing and said he played skillfully and possessed many other traits to bring peace to Saul. That's favor. Whenever evil spirits encroached on Saul, Holy Spirit would take over as David played anointed worship. Saul would be restored, and the spirit would leave. He ultimately made David his armor bearer, had him live in the palace, and made him an army captain of 1,000 (see 1 Sam. 16:18, 23; 18:2, 13). That's favor. Servanthood does something important in and for us. Every destiny journey needs to include servanthood.

Beware: *Of those who enter leadership without a season of servanthood.*

ATTACKS

Anointing also brings attacks. The birds of the air parable says the enemy swoops in to steal our word (see Matt. 13:4, 19), including that which declared our anointing. David understood personally that those who are anointed will also be attacked. After Samuel anointed him, David experienced confusion and hurt by unceasing persecution and unprovoked murder attempts by Saul. Once, when he fled from Saul, he asked Jonathan, "What have I done? What is my iniquity?" (1 Sam. 20:1). He'd ask that question again as he encountered attacks from Saul and others. David hadn't defied or supplanted Saul. He'd been anointed in his place. Unwarranted harassment defies logic because it's not about us but our anointing.

Beware: *Of those who count your anointing as an affront against them.*

David's son, Solomon, commented on how for a season God's chosen may not be in the place of leadership: "I have seen servants riding on horses, while princes walk on the ground like servants" (see Eccles. 10:7). Poet

James Russell Lowell said, "Truth forever on the scaffold, Wrong forever on throne."[4] Sometimes our calling's fruition seems to take forever, and in the meantime someone else may be in on the throne. But though ungodly bosses, dictators, politicians, or other persecutors appear to reign for a season, God's knows how to turn things around. The unrighteous may be in charge today, but the anointing will prevail. God brings us into our proper place because "the triumphing of the wicked is short" (Job 20:5).

Beware: *Of resenting others in leadership when you're anointed for that position.*

David fled for his life from Saul and other enemies because of his calling and anointing. Saul attempted to kill him multiple times because David was to replace him. Absalom and Shimei wanted David's position. The Philistines sought to kill David when they heard he'd "been anointed king over all Israel" (1 Chron. 14:8). They were probably thinking he'd inflicted plenty of damage on them before his official anointing to reign. When he was actually installed as Israel's king, he'd be unbeatable. They also probably considered the damage Israel could inflict now that they were united with Judah. Satan attacks your fruitfulness by attacking order and unity. Unity goes hand-in-hand with anointing and blessings (see Ps. 133:1-3). It's a great destiny weapon against attacks.

Beware: *Of those who attack because of your anointing.*

PROTECTION FROM CHOICES

The anointing was David's covering from enemies. However, the Lord also protected his anointing from another enemy—his poor choices. When David lived in Ziklag and Philistines were going to war, their commanders excluded David because of potential conflict. Like with Saul, David resented the rejection and again asked what he'd done wrong (see 1 Sam. 29:6–8). However, this time God used Philistine leaders for His purpose. They weren't persecuting David but rather unwittingly protecting him. His anointing had brought him favor, attacks, covering, and this time protection from a huge mistake. God doesn't want us to fight against His people, and David would've done that if they battled with Saul. Allying with Philistines

Connie Hunter-Urban

rather than the nation he'd one day rule would've affected his destiny and acceptance as king.

Beware: *Of feeling rejection when God may actually be protecting your calling.*

To make that situation worse, the choice would've surely followed him because in that battle, Philistines killed Saul and his sons (see 1 Sam. 31:6). God's love for David kept him from making a huge mistake. This wasn't the first time God had safeguarded David from committing an act that would later hurt his kinghood. After Nabal refused to provide for David and his men, David readied for an attack. Then, Abigail intervened. If he'd followed through with his anger, he would've been like Saul going after priests at Nob. Killing a fellow Israelite or shedding blood without cause or for vengeance might've affected his kingship (see 1 Sam. 25:26). Our choices determine if God can take us into His plan, so He often safeguards them.

Beware: *Of reacting in anger and making a decision you'll later regret.*

CONCLUSION

The anointing gives much but comes with rewards couched in challenges. God keeps us in spirit, soul, and body through high and low times. He may use an Abigail, Philistine, Jonathan, or Saul to thwart actions that could hurt our destinies. He protects us from errors and enemies that could work against us and later affect promotion. David knew because of his calling and anointing, the Lord would "prepare a table before [him] in the presence of [his] enemies; [and] anoint [his] head with oil" (Ps. 23:5). As a result, like David's cup, ours will be full and running over.

QUESTIONS TO PONDER
(Answers in Appendix)
SHIMEI

1. Why did Shimei perceive David as his enemy?

2. List Shimei's accusations?

3. How did Abishai react to this and other attacks against David?

4. What's the main reason David said not to kill Shimei at this time?

5. What instructions did David leave for Solomon regarding Shimei?

6. How did Solomon deal with Shimei, and how did Shimei violate that?

THE ANOINTING

7. What's the difference between being called and chosen?

8. Give examples of God's choices who weren't the best that man had to offer.

9. Explain the anointing.

10. Give three ways the anointing protects us.

Something to Consider: How does David's enemy/weapon in this chapter speak about our enemies/weapons today?

Part Two

DAVID'S FRIENDS

Chapter Six

JONATHAN

DAVID'S REFLECTIONS

How good and how pleasant it is for brethren to dwell together in unity! (Ps. 133:1)

A necessary weapon of warfare is friends' support. As far back as Eden, God said man needed companionship (see Gen. 2:18). Paul understood that because once he was forlorn at Troas when he couldn't find his friend Titus. Knowing that, he says not to forsake coming together as believers. Christians need the support and accountability of one another. Early in our destiny journeys and beyond, we should foster relationship with God and friends to help us proceed toward the prize and stand beside us in battle. An army isn't comprised of only one person, but victory happens as we work together against satan (see Heb. 10:25; 2 Cor. 2:12–13). David had lots of enemies but also many loyal, gracious, loving friends who were powerful weapons and support.

A FRIEND AND LEADER

Jonathan exemplifies a devoted friend's love. His name means "given of God,"[1] and he was truly God's gift to David. As friends, peers, confidants, and brothers-in-law, they loved and bonded early. After Saul took David home with him and didn't allow him to return to his father, David and

Jonathan became brothers. Jonathan encouraged, protected, loved, and trusted David. As Saul's son, he was the likely successor to the throne, yet he acknowledged God's will for his friend to be king. Though Jonathan didn't live to see his destiny's fruition, his faithfulness to his friend was rewarded through his son. Jonathan's prowess and love for the Lord would've made him a good king. However, his dad's choices changed his destiny.

The first reference to Jonathan was after Saul had been king a while and showed his leadership weakness while his son's skill emerged. Saul chose 3,000 fighting men and put Jonathan in charge of 1,000, a sign of his father's trust in his abilities and leadership. After Jonathan attacked their garrison, Philistines became riled and gathered a massive army. Many from Israel fled, but Saul stayed with his army that had dwindled to 600. Philistines surrounded those who remained. An Israeli victory was highly unlikely with their unequal numbers and weapons. However, despite disadvantages, Hebrews were superior in one great way: their God. They ultimately defeated the Philistines after Jonathan's courage and insight (see 1 Sam. 13:1–6, 17–18). Unlike his dad, Jonathan knew where his strength lay. He said, "It may be that the Lord will work for [them…and will save] by many or few" (1 Sam. 14:6). What a contrast between him and Saul! He knew the battle was the Lord's while Saul did whatever seemed good to him.

Beware: *Of those who discount God's power.*

Jonathan took only his armor bearer toward the Philistines' garrison. Jonathan and the Philistines were positioned between two sharp rocks. He planned to reveal themselves to the Philistines. If they said they'd approach Jonathan, he and the armor bearer wouldn't move toward them. If they said to come up to them, they'd go because that would be a sign the Lord had delivered them to Jonathan. Slyly intending to entrap the Hebrews, the Philistines called for them to approach. Proceeding as God had instructed, Jonathan and his armor bearer crawled surreptitiously and killed about twenty Philistines in half an acre. Jonathan's trust in God was rewarded by the Lord's sending an earthquake to complete Israel's victory (see 1 Sam. 14:1, 4–15). Sometimes, a sparse army populates the front line, but God has the last word.

Beware: *Of thinking winning comes because of mighty numbers or weapons.*

SAUL'S FAULTY LEADERSHIP

After the earthquake, Saul took roll and discovered Jonathan and his armor bearer were gone. He called for the ark (probably an ephod) and priest to get direction then heard increased noise in the Philistine camp. He didn't realize the tumult was because of Jonathan's efforts. At that point, he asked the priest to "Withdraw [his] hand" (1 Sam. 14:19), meaning he didn't let the priest hear from God before he moved to battle. Seeking God's will is good, but this act shows that Saul wasn't truly interested in hearing from Him. He fought the Philistines, who were in such confusion they attacked each other. Others rejoined Saul, so the Philistines fled. The Lord saved Israel that day, thanks in large part to Jonathan's actions. However, Saul had committed a grave error, and his people "were distressed" (1 Sam. 14:24). Not considering demands of battle, he arbitrarily ordered that no one eat until evening after their vengeance on the Philistines. Perhaps he thought fasting was righteous, so God would be pleased with him. However, this hasty order was based on Saul's wishes rather than knowledge of and trust in God's ability (see 1 Sam. 14:17–24).

BEWARE: *Of leaders who make a show of seeking God but don't follow through.*

Saul's ordering them not to eat caused people to sin. Because they were extremely hungry, they rushed on Philistine animals, slaughtered, and then devoured them before pouring the blood on the altar for a sacrifice. This violated God's law. When Saul heard, he had them roll a rock there and bring animals for sacrifice. He intended to plunder the Philistines and not leave anyone alive, so he asked God's direction through the priest. God's response to Saul should be a lesson: He was silent. Saul presumed He didn't answer because of sin in the camp. His assumption of others' guilt rather than his own led to another hasty order—to kill the offender who'd eaten in disregard of his orders (see Lev. 17:12; 1 Sam. 14:31–39).

Beware: *Of leaders whose actions cause others to sin.*

Jonathan had been away and hadn't heard Saul's order. He'd become hungry and dipped his sword into honey dripping from a tree in a forest. The honey's sweetness refreshed him. When someone told Jonathan of his father's command, he demonstrated wisdom and love his dad hadn't shown for the people. He voiced that Saul "ha[d] troubled the land" (1 Sam. 14:29). The word used for "trouble" is the same word used when Joshua asked Achan, "Why have you troubled us?" (Josh. 7:25). It's *akar*, meaning to "disturb or afflict."[2] That kind of trouble is sin; Saul, not Jonathan, had sinned by burdening his people. Jonathan confessed he'd eaten honey without knowing Saul's edict. His dad reacted with his typical lack of wisdom. He intended to kill Jonathan, but others intervened because of his great victory. How ironic that Saul gave leniency to those who rushed on animals in violation of *God's* law but planned to kill his son for disobeying *his* orders (see 1 Sam. 14:27–29, 43–45).

Beware: *Of leaders who believe their wishes are more important than God's.*

SAUL'S BROKEN PROMISES

Jonathan "delighted greatly in David" (1 Sam. 19:1); so when Saul told him and his servants to kill his friend, he couldn't obey his father and king. He informed David that Saul wanted him dead and to stay hidden until morning. Jonathan defended David to Saul and said he'd done good things for the king. Killing him would be shedding innocent blood because no reason existed for the act. Because his son defended David, Saul heeded and swore, "As the Lord lives, he shall not be killed" (1 Sam. 19:6). After Jonathan brokered peace, David returned to Saul as in the past. He went to war against the Philistines and defeated them so badly that they fled. However, Saul didn't celebrate David's victories for Israel but again tried multiple times to kill David, who fled to Jonathan (see 1 Sam. 19:1–10; 20:1).

Beware: *Of believing the word of those whose history shows their word means little.*

Later, Jonathan gave his dad benefit of the doubt and assured David that Saul wouldn't do anything before he told his son. However, David knew that with Saul, "there [was] but a step between [him] and death" (1

Sam. 20:3). When David said Saul might not tell Jonathan of his plans because of their closeness, he suggested that during the feast of the New Moon, he'd hide instead of eating with Saul. If Saul asked, Jonathan should say he'd gone to be with family. Saul's anger or acceptance would show his intentions. They made a plan for how they would communicate (see 1 Sam. 20:2, 5–7). Jonathan's care for David was a blessing from a friend, who provided necessary help and saved David's life. Perhaps Solomon thought of that friendship when he penned, "The righteous should choose his friends carefully, for the way of the wicked leads them astray" (Prov. 12:26).

Beware: *Of not recognizing friends as God's mighty weapons.*

While David hid, Jonathan and Abner sat by Saul at dinner. The first day the king didn't question David's empty seat. However, the second day when he asked Jonathan why David didn't attend, Jonathan answered that he'd gone to Bethlehem. Livid, Saul accused Jonathan of choosing David over him and called Jonathan and his mother names. He pointed out that if David lived, Jonathan wouldn't be king and ordered him to fetch David so he could kill him. When Jonathan asked why he deserved death, Saul threw a spear to kill his son. Jonathan then knew David's fate. He angrily left the table and ate nothing because of grief about his father's shameful treatment of his friend. The next morning, he returned to the field and signaled David, who emerged from hiding, fell on his face, and bowed three times. He and Jonathan kissed each other and wept. Jonathan told him to go in peace and mentioned their covenant. With heavy hearts, the two friends parted, not knowing if they'd see one another again or if Saul would relent from his murderous obsession (see 1 Sam. 20:24–35, 41–42).

Beware: *Of those whose violent reaction shows their heart.*

LOVE

His earthly father had lost his way, but Jonathan did whatever his heavenly Father wanted. Despite Saul's pursuit of David, his friend came again to reassure him of his place in God's plan. God provided much-needed encouragement when Jonathan guaranteed him his dad wouldn't find him and his destiny was assured as Israel's next king. This was a true display of love. Love prefers others, like Jonathan demonstrated although he realized his friend's promotion would mean his forfeiture of kingship. Jesus said not only to love God but our neighbors as much as we love ourselves (see Matt. 22:37–39). Having His heart of love makes us develop others' callings, often even more than our own. Loving, preferring others, and not living for self alone should be our character. When we're preoccupied with *self*, we miss opportunities to be God's representative.

True love operates "without hypocrisy" (Rom. 12:9), and Jonathan personified this. His allying with David would alienate his irrational dad; but, still, he loved "fervently with a pure heart" (1 Pet. 1:22). Jonathan's love saved his friend and God's choice of king. He promised David that Saul wouldn't find him and that everyone, even his father, knew David would "be Israel's king" (see 1 Sam. 23:17). He accepted that truth, accommodated it, and vowed to serve beside David. He didn't compare his destiny with David's or bemoan his loss after his friend's promotion. Instead, his love for God and David made him delight in doing God's will and encouraging David (see 1 Sam. 23:16–17). What a display of love for David and God! Do we demonstrate His love and selflessness when dealing with others, or do we seek our advancement despite God's will?

eware: *Of those who make choices for their own advantage.*

COVENANT

Covenant is a serious vow. When David faced Goliath, he resented the giant thinking he could defeat God's children with whom He had covenant. After Goliath's defeat, "the soul of Jonathan [had been] knit to the soul of David, and Jonathan…and David made a covenant" (1 Sam. 18:1, 3). As a show of faith, Jonathan gave David his robe, armor, sword, bow, and belt (see 1 Sam. 18:4). Perhaps he knew even then that David was God's choice for king, so he bequeathed his friend these symbols of his kingship. This was another demonstration of Jonathan's unselfish nature, his ultimate show of friendship, and his love for David and the Father. Jesus said the greatest example of love was a friend willing to lay down his life for a friend (see John

15:13). Jonathan laid down everything that would've been his own destiny and demonstrated integrity his father lacked. Later, David reiterated the oath not to "cut off [his] kindness from [Jonathan's] house forever" (1 Sam. 20:15). He never forgot these covenants with Saul and Jonathan when he said, "May the Lord be between you and me, and between your descendants and my descendants, forever" (1 Sam. 20:42). David later even honored Saul's broken covenant with the Gibeonites (see 2 Sam. 21:1).

One major covenant in Scripture is the Davidic Covenant. This is also referred to as the "covenant of salt" (2 Chron. 13:5) Because of its use in sacrifices and preservative nature, salt symbolized God's everlasting covenant.[3] God promised to give Israel a permanent location, make David a house, and establish his seed and throne of his kingdom forever (see 2 Sam. 7:10–13). Later allusions to this covenant said David would always have a man on Israel's throne (see Jer. 33:17), and that covenant was referred to as the "sure mercies of David" (Isa. 55:3). Jesus also spoke those words (see Acts 13:34). That covenant's fulfillment happened by His birth, death, and resurrection.

HONORING COVENANTS

Covenants mean something, and David fulfilled his covenants. After a time as Israel's king, he asked if any of Saul's house was still alive so he could show kindness because of Jonathan (see 2 Sam. 9:1). They called Saul's former servant, Ziba, who said Jonathan's lame son, Mephibosheth, was alive. When Saul and Jonathan had died, he was five. After news of their deaths, Mephibosheth fell when his nurse had picked him up to escape. He was now living in Machir's house in Lo Debar. He'd been mentioned at Ishbosheth's death, probably because his physical ailments prevented his ruling (see 2 Sam. 9:1–4; 4:4).

Beware: *Of neglecting to honor covenants.*

Unaware of his dad and David's covenant, Mephibosheth was afraid when the king summoned him. He'd probably heard his grandfather's rants about David and had drawn inaccurate conclusions, so he feared the king would kill him. During that era, incoming kings often killed their predecessors' families.[4] Although Mephibosheth wasn't able to rule, he had a son who could pose a threat to David's throne. With negative possibilities of why the king would call for him, Mephibosheth approached David warily and fell before him. David told him not to be afraid because he would show kindness for Jonathan's sake, restore Saul's land, and allow Mephibosheth to eat at David's table. The fear and uncertainty Mephibosheth had felt a few moments earlier were replaced with wonder and confusion. Why would David honor someone with no value? Saul's grandson's life had purpose and honor because of Jonathan and David's covenant. Though Jonathan had passed away before seeing his or David's destinies, his son's destiny was to eat at the king's table. Doesn't that sound like our King, who covenanted with Himself to bless us? He bestows good things on us and asks us to sit at His table (see 2 Sam. 9:6–8).

Beware: *Of feeling unworthy when the King summons you.*

ZIBA

David told Ziba he'd given Mephibosheth all of Saul's property. Ziba and his fifteen sons and twenty servants would be Mephibosheth's servants, work the land, and bring in harvests. However, he'd eat at David's table. Ziba seemed agreeable with this arrangement, but he must've been irritated that the king would honor this cripple of no value. Later, he demonstrated his true feelings. After David had fled from Absalom, he was past the mountaintop when Ziba met him. He had two donkeys, 200 loaves of bread, 100 clusters of raisins, 100 summer fruits, and one skin of wine. When the king asked about Mephibosheth, Ziba said he stayed in Jerusalem, implying he supported Absalom. He claimed Mephibosheth had commented that this day the kingdom would be restored to him. David believed Ziba and gave him all Mephibosheth possessed (see 2 Sam. 9:9–12; 16:1–4).

After David returned to Jerusalem, Mephibosheth approached the king. He hadn't cared for his appearance since David had left. When the king asked why he hadn't gone with him, he said Ziba had promised to ride to David because of Mephibosheth's lameness. However, Ziba had deceived David by slandering Mephibosheth with untrue words. Mephibosheth compared David to an "angel of God" (2 Sam. 19:27) and trusted David to do what he felt was right. He repeated what David had done for Jonathan's household although he could've killed them. Mephibosheth's appearance, humility, and gratitude lent credibility to his version and his loyalty. David didn't attempt to determine the truth but said he and Ziba could divide the land. Mephibosheth said to give everything to Ziba because he was blessed that David was back (see 2 Sam. 19:24–30).

Beware: *Of those with ulterior motives who provide information.*

CONCLUSION

God has given many tools and weapons for destiny, and friends are a big part of that. They guide and defend us. They let us know when evil approaches and accommodate our success while at times sacrificing their own advancements. David's son said, "A friend loves at all times, and a brother is born for adversity" (Prov. 17:17). David's friend and brother arrived when David could've given up on his destiny. God knows how to keep us on the destiny track He prepared.

DAVID'S WEAPONS: RELATIONSHIP AND HIS PRESENCE

DAVID'S REFLECTIONS

[In the Wilderness of Judah] When I remember You on my bed, I meditate on You in the night watches. Because You have been my help, therefore in the shadow of Your wings I will rejoice. My soul follows close behind You; Your right hand upholds me. (Ps. 63:6–8)

RELATIONSHIP

The powerful weapon of relationship is one most Christians don't employ because they're satisfied with religion rather than relationship. Children, spouse, and friends all know us, and we know them intimately because of time together. Occasions with the Father produce the same outcomes. We develop relationship by spending time and communicating with Him. When He first speaks to you, you're unsure if He's actually talking. However, the more you communicate, the more you know even His whisper. I once heard a speaker say we can become pregnant with God's plans, but only with intimacy. When David met Goliath, the Philistines, or murderous Saul, he had an advantage—he understood relationship. His obsession with the Lord's presence made God say while he was a boy, "I have found David the son of Jesse, a man after My own heart, who will do all My will" (Acts 13:22). If we don't spend time with Him, we won't know Him. We understand His heart through relationship, and that makes us destiny-ready.

Samuel also exemplifies relationship. The first time God spoke to him, he was young and didn't recognize His voice because at that time, "Samuel did not yet know the LORD, nor was the word of the Lord yet revealed to him" (1 Sam. 3:7). That statement is unbelievable! He was dedicated to God before conception. He lived in the tabernacle and was mentored by Israel's priest and judge. He performed temple duties but didn't know God. These dynamics sound like many today. They go to church, work for God, become trained by great seminaries and religious leaders, but they don't "yet know the Lord." They never sought relationship and intimacy. After God called Samuel's name and he listened, circumstances changed. Because of relationship he could hear from the Father when Eli couldn't. As a result, God "let none of his words fall to the ground" (1 Sam. 3:19). David and Samuel both found out as boys that fostering relationship with God creates a destiny pathway.

SOLITARY SEASONS

David trusted God to fulfill his purpose and fight his battles because of relationship he'd gained during isolated times on the hillsides. Therefore, don't despise your solitary seasons. My husband's former pastor used to say, "The consolation of isolation is revelation." Because of solitary seasons, David became confident in God's ability to guide him through attacks and then to his destiny, no matter who or what enemy arose or how difficult the journey. He realized that when circumstances became dire, he could trust God because he'd gained dependence on Him long before he became a political or military icon. He said, "The secret of the LORD is with those who fear Him.... My eyes are ever toward the LORD, for He shall pluck my feet out of the net" (Ps. 25:14–15). Those with shared secrets have intimacy and confidence in their covenant of protection. Part of destiny training should include nurturing that intimacy with our Father.

Beware: *Of not recognizing the necessity of solitary seasons.*

Learning more about Him brings relationship and power. During various seasons, each experience that requires calling upon Him once more intensifies the connection that will assist us as we move into destiny. Dismal circumstances—our Goliaths, Ziklags, or Adullams—change through relationship. Knowledge comes as we desire the Giver, not just His gifts. No matter who or what confronts us, relationship allows us to see victory from God's eyes. He says, "Because he has set his love upon Me, therefore I will deliver him; I will set him on high, because he has known My name. He shall call upon Me, and I will answer him; I will be with him in trouble; I will deliver him and honor him" (Ps. 91:14–15). Solitary seasons build relationship and thus confidence that God does know our names and everything else about us. He'll be with us and lead us to victory.

CONFIDENCE

Certainty in God comes through realizing we can't do anything without Him (see John 15:5). As we draw closer, Jesus' "strength is made perfect in [our] weakness" (2 Cor. 12:9). David understood how to rest in the Lord during darkest times. He was betrayed by his son. His life was in jeopardy while that son and others pursued. While he fled, Shimei viciously attacked his character and person. During these great sorrows, he said, "I lay down and slept; I awoke, for the LORD sustained me" (Ps. 3:5). Though Absalom sought his life and Shimei railed against him, David and his men rested "and refreshed themselves there" (2 Sam. 16:14), in the midst of the storm in Shimei's territory. At this terrible time, he had peace and trust that God would keep watch over him (see 2 Sam. 16:5, 14). Often, our bodies need rest because the enemy's tactics are to wear us out (see Dan. 7:25), physically, mentally, and spiritually. However, like David, we can lie down in peace because God's responsible for our safety (see Ps. 4:8).

Jesus also demonstrated confidence during the storm. While disciples feared the turbulence of boisterous waves, Jesus was "asleep on a pillow" (Mark 4:38). Isn't that thrilling? Even our Lord needed rest, and that vicious storm with its lightning and booming thunder didn't disturb His sleep. If life's storms didn't consume or steal sleep from David nor Jesus, why should we fret when we encounter them? As a bonus, Jesus will be with you in the tempest. Mary forged relationship at His feet; so when life's gales brought her brother's death, she approached the Master and got a resurrection (see John 11:32, 44). Because their strength was in the Lord, they rested during the worst of storms. With relationship, He's our essence in all our moves, decisions, breaths, rest. We gladly relinquish our will to His and understand He's in control.

OUR THINKING

Relationship lets us see beyond circumstances because we understand His faithfulness. Part of forging relationship with God is to change *stinkin' thinkin'* that says we're defeated rather than believing we're overcomers. Then, our outlook changes from victim to victor. Relationship lets us know we're "the head and not the tail...above...and not...beneath" (Deut. 28:13). David could've easily and legitimately wallowed often in self-pity. Instead, he knew God and realized persecution was for a greater purpose. Like he experienced after his moral failure with Bathsheba, sin causes us to lose our peace and desire the return of our salvation's joy (see Ps. 51:12). Relationship allows us to rise above even our mistakes and know we'll prevail because of Him.

The wilderness experience showed how being close to God or continuing in stinkin' thinkin' affects destiny. Although other prophets heard from the Lord, God described Moses as one who communicated with Him "face to face" (Num. 12:8). In contrast, the people didn't seek relationship but knew God through Moses. When they left Egypt, they retained a victim mentality. At the Red Sea, things looked bad with the Egyptian army bearing down behind them and the enormous Red Sea in front. Without relationship, people hadn't caught the vision of what God wanted for their nation, and they never did. Does that sound like today? Some want to be part of a new move of God; but with each step into new territory and every ordeal, they complain and criticize. At their first trial, they scolded Moses, saying, "It would have been better for us to serve the Egyptians than that we should die in the wilderness" (Exod. 14:12). They longed for flesh pots and onions but forgot the terrible work conditions, beatings, or babies ordered to be drowned in the Nile. Moses heard and took their complaints to God. Without intimacy with Him, we often desire to return to our land of hatred, abuse, and servitude like a "dog returns to his own vomit" or "a sow, having washed, to her wallowing in the mire" (2 Pet. 2:22). Because of relationship, Moses knew the Father would come through, and He did time and again. Relationship propels us toward purpose and gives confidence and abilities once we arrive.

GOD'S PRESENCE

Relationship comes through being in God's presence. David was a man who desired "One thing... [to] dwell in the house of the Lord" (Ps. 27:4). He was addicted to God's presence, but he wasn't the only one. Moses told God that if His presence didn't go with them, not to send them elsewhere (see Exod. 33:15). In the psalm he authored, Moses said the Lord had been where all generations had dwelt (see Ps. 90:1). Another psalmist said that one day in God's presence has more value than a thousand days outside of it (see Ps. 84:10). We draw close to God by pursuing His presence.

His presence changes us and thus destiny. Isaiah spent time with God and may have been thinking of David when he said God "dwell[s] in the high and holy place, with him who has a contrite and humble spirit" (Isa. 57:15). Praise and worship in humility usher us into His presence. With regular appointments, we approach, not with hands out, but up. We climb onto His lap with no agenda but to love and welcome Him with adoration. In His presence, we lay our heads on His breast and get to know Him—His face, voice, breath, whispers, thoughts, heart. After the temple's completion, God's presence was so thick that at times priests couldn't minister (see 1 Kings 8:10–11). That likely occurred because of David's and his son's passion for God's presence.

SECRET PLACE

While Saul persecuted David, Jonathan told David to hide in his "secret place" (1 Sam. 19:2). When we go to our secret place, God protects, directs, and shares His secrets. David understood the power of that place. During trouble, the Lord hid him "in the secret place of His tabernacle... [and] set [him] high upon a rock" as his (Ps. 27:5). In that secret hiding place, God protects and delivers while bringing perfect peace. We don't fret but rather realize he who "dwells in the secret place of the Most High shall abide under the shadow of the Almighty" (Ps. 91:1). The word, "dwells," is *yashab*, "to sit down... remain...settle...marry."[1] Dwelling in that secret place isn't a temporary fix but a lifestyle of staking our claim under God's shadow.

Beware: *Of those who neglect their secret place.*

The secret place of God's presence houses great blessings. One night we were preparing to do a streaming program at our house when Randy showed up. He had such painful varicose veins in his legs, he was sometimes unable to work. He'd been prayed for often, but healing had eluded him. That night, he sat on our stairs while others gathered around him. I felt led to worship, singing about Jehovah Rapha, Randy's Healer. Suddenly we felt the Lord's presence intensely as our worship ushered us into the secret place. The anointing was so strong I had difficulty staying upright on the piano bench. His manifestation accomplished what it was sent for—Randy's legs were healed. Our secret place where God's presence dwells is a powerful weapon against the enemy.

THE ARK

Eli had died after hearing about his sons' deaths and the Philistine capture of the ark. His pregnant daughter-in-law mourned the ark's loss, in addition to her father-in-law and husband's deaths. She said, "The glory has departed from Israel, for the ark of God has been captured" (1 Sam. 4:22). She grieved so intensely her son was born; she named him Ichabod, meaning "no glory."[2] Her child's name and her words show her deep sorrow about the loss of God's presence. It had remained gone from Jerusalem since before Samuel became judge, and Saul didn't see the necessity for God's presence while he was king. As a matter of fact, the nation hadn't even inquired about the ark during his reign. King David didn't follow Saul's model of not bringing it back. He loved the Lord with all his heart and had a passion for His presence. He made preparations to bring the ark back to Jerusalem. David's retrieving it showed Israel that he cherished God's presence (see 1 Sam. 4:17, 21; 1 Chron. 13:1–4). We should emulate him to value God's presence more than anything. Then we can truly repeat David's words: "Lord, I have loved the habitation of your house" (Ps. 26:8).

Beware: *Of being satisfied to live without God's presence.*

David gathered 30,000 of Israel's best men to bring it back on a new cart from Abinadab's house. Uzzah and Ahio, Abinadab's sons, drove the cart. Ahio went before it while David and all Israel played instruments. On the way back, the oxen stumbled, so Uzzah extended his hand to steady the ark. Perhaps Uzzah did this because he'd grown up with an appreciation for God's presence. However, just like the men at Beth Shemesh had illegally looked inside (see 1 Sam. 6:19), both Uzzah's and David's actions were disobedient to God's law. The ark wasn't to be carried on a cart but by poles on Levites' shoulders, and no one was to touch it (see Exod. 25:14–15; Num. 4:15). That tells me that a new move of God's presence should come on priests' shoulders, and it shouldn't be about human effort. Once again, David got into trouble when he proceeded without consulting God. By the time Solomon moved the ark into the temple, he understood the process (see 2 Sam. 6:1–6; 1 Kings 8:6).

Beware: *Of doing God's work without His direction.*

Since David hadn't sought how to transport it, God punished them, despite Uzzah's intention to protect the ark. In His anger, the Lord struck him dead. This seems like punishment for doing something good. That's probably why David grew indignant and called that place Perez Uzzah, "against Uzzah" (2 Sam. 6:8). However, he didn't stay angry or discouraged but remained determined to recover it, despite this failure. Getting God's presence back in Jerusalem was too important, but he realized God's will must be sought. While he questioned how to return it, the ark remained at Obed-Edom's house for three months. During that time, God blessed Obed Edom, his entire household, and all he had (see 1 Chron. 15:13; 2 Sam. 6:8–9, 11).

Beware: *Of violating God's precepts even for a good reason.*

When David heard about Obed-Edom's blessings, he was even more zealous for God's presence. He took elders and captains to bring the ark back. He discovered the appropriate mode of transportation then had heads of the Levites' houses sanctify themselves. To demonstrate his respect, he involved the entire nation and used his resources "with gladness" (2 Sam. 6:12). He asked Levite leaders to appoint singers, accompanied by instruments. They raised voices with "resounding joy" (see 1 Chron. 15:16). People walked six paces and sacrificed (see 2 Sam. 6:13). Solomon would mirror his dad's love for God's presence and also sacrifice when he transported the ark to the temple—"sheep and oxen that could not be counted or numbered for multitude" (1 Kings 8:5). How do we use our resources: money, time, energy, thoughts? Are we like Solomon and David, who used their best to procure God's presence? Do we understand His presence is crucial as we perform God-given tasks that groom us for what comes next in our journey?

David had prepared a tent for the ark after its return. When they arrived in Jerusalem and put it in David's tabernacle, he appointed Levites to minister and worship before it and chose others for tabernacle jobs. They sang, and David shared Israel's history (see Ps. 105). He made burnt and peace offerings and blessed the people in God's name. Asaph and his brothers were to worship regularly before the ark while others played instruments. Zadok, the priest, and his brothers were gatekeepers and gave offerings morning and evening. Zadok's line subsequently had charge of the altar (see Ezek. 40:16). Obed-Edom and his sixty-eight brothers also became gatekeepers. I love that detail. Obed Edom had three months of dwelling with the ark. After that experience, the whole family was addicted to God's presence and left their homes to work in the tabernacle. Once we've regularly experienced His presence, we can't live without it (see 1 Chron. 16:1, 4–6, 37–42). It's crucial to our growth in Him.

CONCLUSION

Like God's presence brought destiny to Obed Edom's family, being in His presence changes us while moving us forward. After you spend time with the Lord, you'll desire his presence like David did. God's presence comes because of relationship. David said, "You will show me the path of life; in Your presence is fullness of joy; at Your right hand are pleasures forevermore" (Ps. 16:11). If we seek His presence, the journey to destiny and beyond will be of great value.

QUESTIONS TO PONDER
JONATHAN

1. How did the Lord "save by many or by few" for Jonathan?

2a. Why was Saul going to kill Jonathan?

2b. How did that show his heart and priorities?

3. Give examples of how Jonathan showed friendship and love to David.

4. Explain covenant.

5a. Tell Mephibosheth's story.

5b. How did Ziba slander Mephibosheth?

RELATIONSHIP and HIS PRESENCE

6. What does God accomplish in us during solitary seasons?

7. What does the author mean by "stinkin' thinkin'"?

8. Explain the difference between Moses and other prophets.

9. What was David's "one thing"?

10. Describe the "secret place."

Something to Consider: How do David's friend/weapons in this chapter speak about our friends/weapons today?

Chapter Seven

SIGNIFICANT PROPHETS

DAVID'S REFLECTIONS

[After Nathan confronted him about Uriah] Purge me with hyssop, and I shall be clean; wash me, and I shall be whiter than snow. Make me hear joy and gladness, that the bones You have broken may rejoice. Hide Your face from my sins, and blot out all my iniquities. (Ps. 51:7–9)

SAMUEL

Samuel represents those who can hear from God on issues as important as the nation's fate. Having someone prophesy your calling then mentor you is crucial for warfare and destiny. One author of the books of Samuel, he was a judge, prophet, and priest. First mentioned at his birth, he became a great part of Israel when he lived with Eli. His name means "heard of God; asked of God."[1] That describes his beginnings, both when his mother pleaded for a child and when God communicated with him as a child. He was a great prophetic weapon on David's behalf, and they were similar in many ways. As children, they both heard from the Lord and obeyed God and those with rule over them. They both grieved for Saul at different times. Both men of prayer, Samuel prayed all night after God told him about stripping the kingdom from Saul (see 1 Sam. 3:4; 15:11), and David prayed on many occasions. While a child, "the Lord was with [Samuel].... And all Israel... knew that Samuel had been established as a prophet" (1 Sam. 3:19–20). David's success would also be attributed to that fact—"the LORD was with him" (1 Sam. 18:14).

The story of Samuel's birth inspires many. His mother, Hannah, had long awaited a child, but God had a purpose and timing for her destiny to birth Israel's greatest and final judge. Often, trials foster patience as we wait rather than plunge in. Many benefits come from patience. For example, "those who wait on the Lord shall renew their strength" (Isa. 40:31). David said waiting brings strength to our hearts (see Ps. 27:14). Waiting is powerful as we prepare for God's purpose, and we can't get in a hurry or grow weary while we wait. The writer of Hebrews lists many who had promises that took a long time to come to pass, but they remained confident that God was faithful (see Gal. 6:9; Heb. 11). Sometimes the answer to our prayers and fulfillment of destiny is on the way, but its fruition must be on God's timetable to accomplish His purpose. Even God's Son was born "when the fullness of the time had come" (Gal. 4:4). During the season when we don't see our answer, we must trust God's faithfulness to birth our Samuels. Hannah, because of her promise, dedicated her son to the Lord's service in the temple. He lived with and studied under Eli where he ministered as a child (see 1 Sam. 2:18). Samuel's destiny journey had begun early, but he had much to learn before he could be ready for its fulfilment.

TO HAVE A KING

Little is recorded about Samuel for the twenty years of his upbringing until Eli died; then he stepped into his destiny as Israel's leader. As a prophet, he judged Israel the rest of his life, even after Saul became king (see 1 Sam. 7:15). He was brought into the world to deal with important issues of his day. Politically, transitioning from a nation of judges to being ruled by a king required God's best facilitator. Spiritually, he was needed to restore national relationship with God. During Eli's time, "the word of the Lord was rare...; there was no widespread revelation" (1 Sam. 3:1). Samuel would change that because he heard from God often. He would anoint Saul as the first king until David was older and better prepared to be tapped as God's true choice of king. Because Hannah awaited her promise, Samuel was born so he would be the man God needed for that time. God wants to birth the extraordinary in us; often we, too, must wait.

Beware: *Of impatience to birth God's will in His time.*

Samuel had judged Israel well but had grown old, so he made his sons judges. Like Eli's sons, his were evil, with no regard for God's ways. They "turned aside after dishonest gain, took bribes, and perverted justice" (1 Sam. 8:3). Their lack of integrity made others balk at their being judges. This principle is crucial as we prepare for destiny: Character matters. These sons could've continued their father's amazing legacy, but they never purged traits that disqualified them for their positions. As a result, people wanted a king. Years before, Moses had prophesied that Israel would want a king like other nations, and it occurred in Samuel's time (Deut. 17:14). Although change is often a good thing, transforming because of what other nations do is wrong. Following man's way rather than God's has consequences. That request grieved both Samuel and God and showed Samuel's human side—disappointment, anger, hurt (see 1 Sam. 8:1–6). God knew his feelings and told him, "they have not rejected you, but they have rejected Me, that I should not reign over them" (1 Sam. 8:7). What a sad statement, yet how amazing that God wanted to comfort Samuel about his feelings of rejection!

Beware: *Of pursuing what you want even after God has clearly spoken.*

That should give perspective about how to respond when others don't receive our God-given words. It should also teach about self-serving choices. When we go our own way or don't receive others' legitimate prophetic words, we're rejecting God. He told Samuel to warn people of negative aspects of having a king then demonstrated His displeasure at their request. Although the rainy season didn't occur during wheat harvest,[2] at Saul's coronation Samuel called to the Lord who sent thunder and rain. People became frightened of Samuel and God and asked not to die for the sin of wanting a king (see 1 Sam. 8:9; 12:17–19).

BEWARE: *Of feeling rejected when someone ignores God's word through us.*

The Israelites said they wanted a king to "go out before [them] to fight [their] battles" (1 Sam. 8:20). This implied that a king, not God, would lead them to victory and that they didn't whole-heartedly trust the Lord. Pulling away from God and following idols had been their pattern throughout history. That attitude is a prescription for trouble. God told Samuel that from the day they'd come from Egypt until then, they'd rejected God in favor of other gods. Once they got a king, their current idol, his behavior would make them regret that choice. Do we reject God as we serve our idols—homes, jobs, marriages, alcohol, leaders? He wants to be first in our lives, and that means surrendering to His will. As warriors for the kingdom, we must seek God's perfect will, not just what's good or acceptable (see Rom. 1 Sam. 8:11; 12:2). Living in His perfect will brings His perfect destiny.

Beware: *Of elevating idols above God.*

Little record exists of Samuel and David's interactions after he was anointed because Samuel died while Saul was ruling. When God sent Samuel to Jesse's house, he knew Saul had potential for persecution or destruction because when God told him to anoint one of Jesse's sons, he said Saul would kill him if he heard about it. Priests' murders did occur when Saul ordered the massacre at Nob. He later advised David when Saul began his persecution and murder attempts. After Samuel died, Israel gathered, lamented, and buried him at his home in Ramah (see 1 Sam. 16:2; 25:1). Although face-to-face meetings were limited, he and David had a deep spiritual connection. His wisdom and ability to hear from God was crucial to both of their destinies.

NATHAN

Nathan was another of David's weapons of warfare to further his destiny. He represents those whom God puts into our lives to stand by us and speak truth, even harsh words. He was a trusted prophet and adviser for much of David's reign. First mentioned when the king told him he wanted to build God's house, his name means "given; giving; rewarded,"[3] which describes his role of giving advice to David. Later, his, Samuel's, and Gad's writings in the book of Nathan the prophet, about David's and Solomon's reigns, were a source for the Chronicles.[4] Nathan not only outlived David but survived long enough to write about Solomon's reign. Gad and Nathan were mentioned during Hezekiah's reign when they restored the temple according to David's parameters from the Lord through these prophets (see 2 Chron. 9:29; 29:25).

DAVID'S SIN

David's worst decision while he was king involved Nathan. Israel was at war with Ammon. In the spring when kings were supposed to go to battle, David stepped out of godly order and stayed in Jerusalem instead of going with his army. Perhaps he remained home since Syrians were no longer helping the Ammonites, so he felt he wouldn't be needed. Maybe he'd allowed the years of being king to make him feel entitled to skip the battle. Whatever the reason, he neglected his God, job, family, and country by not leading his men in war. Our destiny doesn't have an expiration. We can't stay away from battle; our jobs as kings and priests require us to be on the front line. When we're not in God's will, we become prey to the enemy's wiles. David's remaining in Jerusalem created the opportunity for the Bathsheba encounter (see 2 Sam. 10:19; 11:1), a dark stain on his destiny and legacy.

Beware: *Of stepping out of God's will and opening a door for sin.*

From his roof one night, David surveyed Jerusalem. He spotted a woman bathing, but that description was unclear whether she was totally undressed or just bathing parts of her body. She was beautiful, so David asked about her. When he discovered she was not only married but the wife and daughter of two of his mighty men, he should've been dissuaded from pursuing a liaison. Instead, he "sent messengers and took her" (2 Sam. 11:4). This wording could imply that David *took* her against her will. Though we don't know the dynamics of this incident, a sexual encounter occurred and ended in pregnancy (see 2 Sam. 11:2–5).

Beware: *Of choices that make you fall prey to sin.*

After David heard of Bathsheba's pregnancy, he plotted to keep his sin hidden. By God's law both he and Bathsheba could've been killed, so he concocted a plan and asked Joab to send her husband Uriah to him. After he inquired about the war's progress, he sent Uriah home to wash his feet, eat, and be with his wife so he would appear to be the baby's father. Instead, Uriah slept at the door of the king's house with servants. When David asked why, he said, "The ark and Israel and Judah are dwelling in tents, and my lord Joab and the servants over my lord are encamped in the open fields. Shall I then go to my house to eat and drink, and to lie with my wife?" (2 Sam. 11:11). His integrity and sense of fairness were admirable and a contrast to David during this time, but Uriah's outstanding character sealed his fate. David told Uriah he could go back the next day, but he gave him food and wine to get him drunk. He still slept with David's servants, not with Bathsheba. Because he hadn't succumbed to the king's attempts to divert suspicion, David took more drastic measures (see 2 Sam. 11:6–13; Lev. 20:10).

BEWARE: *Of lust that wants what it wants despite consequences to others.*

SIN

Sin is a persistent foe, endeavoring at every twist and turn to derail destiny. The enemy finds each crack through which he can gain entrance. Temptation is inevitable for everyone. Sin isn't. Regularly, "each one is tempted when he is drawn away by his own desires and enticed" (James 1:14). Enticements may be couched in seemingly innocent acts: conversations, gossip, staring at another man's wife. When we first feel temptation, we should flee circumstances, places, and people who may create an opportunity to fall. We must "have no fellowship with the unfruitful works of darkness, but rather expose them" (Eph. 5:11). Sometimes things to be exposed are in others, but often that darkness is in ourselves. Exposure of darkness to light enables us to overcome temptation's grasp.

If not careful, anyone can fall (1 Cor. 10:12). You, me, King David. We may think we're strong enough to withstand temptations and remain in potentially harmful situations. However, the enemy is crafty and always on the prowl to find those he can "devour," so we must steadfastly resist him when he shows up with his wiles (1 Pet. 5:8–9). We can't avoid thoughts he puts in our minds, but we can decide if we dwell or act on them. During his sin with Bathsheba, David sank into the trap where many fall. He let his eye look then linger on something that wasn't his. We should especially "flee sexual immorality" (1 Cor. 6:18) and beware of "the lust of the flesh [and] eyes, and the pride of life" (1 John 2:16). Lust can be in anyone; when it's pondered over, sin is born. However, if we walk continually in the Spirit, we avoid fleshly lusts. If we don't flee, we can look, linger, lust, sin, then try to cover that failure (see 2 Sam. 11:15). If David had fled, he would've endured much less sorrow. He became his own enemy and reaped an enemy's consequences. His sin created a negative impact on his nation and family, plus other relationships he later mourned. His destiny was also stained. When we surrender to sin, irreparable harm occurs.

Beware: *Of staying in, then acting on temptation.*

NATHAN'S ROLE

Nathan appeared after David's sins of adultery and murder. God waited at least nine months to take David to task. He seemed to have gotten away with everything, "but the thing that David had done displeased the Lord" (2 Sam. 11:27). After the child was born, Nathan brought a word from the Lord. He spoke in a parable about a rich man who took a poor man's sole, beloved lamb because he didn't want to waste his own. David reacted indignantly. He said that rich man had no compassion and must die and return four-fold for the injustice. Unfortunately, David had become so hardened to his sin that he didn't recognize himself in the story. When the enemy deceives, we become oblivious to how bad our sin really is. It often takes a prophet speaking God's hard words in love to make us recognize the depth of our actions. After David's response, Nathan told him, "You are the man!" (2 Sam. 12:7). He'd taken another man's only sheep (Bathsheba) then slaughtered that man (Uriah). He reminded David of all God had done to establish him. He said God would've given him more, but he had wanted Uriah's wife and killed him through Ammon's sword (see 2 Sam. 12:1–9). After Nathan pronounced God's judgment, David asked God to "wash [him] thoroughly from [his] iniquity, and cleanse [him] from [his] sin" (Ps. 51:2).

Beware: *Of thinking you've gotten away with evil.*

Often, people "follow their own desires and…look for teachers who will tell them whatever their itching ears want to hear" (2 Tim. 4:3 New Living Translation). Many who operate in the prophetic or speak God's word are too interested in pleasing others. Those who avoid speaking God's hard words are demonstrating disobedience. However, when God uses us as an instrument of correction for others, we should deliver the message in love, not with a goal to destroy. Hard words and tough love aren't popular and will be met with derision, but voicing them is God's will. Like when Samuel and Nathan were called to give truth to the kings, prophetic integrity means speaking exactly what God has said. This intense confrontation was actually God's and Nathan's love for David. Because Nathan had courage and integrity to speak God's message honestly, David realized the depth of what he'd done. He didn't respond to the prophet's word like Saul had done by blaming others for his sins. Instead, he repented and admitted his guilt. God forgave David's sin, so Nathan said God wouldn't kill him. However, consequences would occur. This sexual sin became an open door to allow perversions and much sorrow for David's family (see 2 Sam. 12:13–14).

CONSEQUENCES

Nathan's pronouncement aligned with God's law that He would "visit the father's iniquity to the third and fourth generation" (see Exod. 20:5). Those generational curses followed people until Jesus eradicated them by becoming the curse Himself (see Gal. 3:13). We now don't have to bear sins that have come through our bloodlines. However, consequences for actions may still happen. For David, his failure brought much sorrow.

- The sword remained in his house and hacked through his family unit.
  - He lost several sons—his newborn with Bathsheba, Amnon, Absalom, Adonijah, and others like Daniel whose birth was recorded but who were not among his sons at the end of his life.
- Adversity would attack from his house.
  - Amnon, Absalom, and Adonijah rebelled.
- He'd lose wives to his neighbor, and they'd lie with his wives in front of everyone. Though he'd sinned in secret, God's judgment would be revealed to all Israel.
  - Absalom bedded his concubines in front of Israel, and the nation was involved in the turmoil of his revolt (see 2 Sam. 12:10–12; 16:22; 15:13).

The hardest consequence was that Bathsheba's child would die because the event caused enemies to blaspheme God. To intercede, David pleaded with God, fasted, lay on the ground all night, and didn't eat or rise. The baby died on the seventh day. Bathsheba conceived again, and they ultimately had four sons together. God sent Nathan after Solomon's birth to tell David to call him Jedidiah (see 1 Chron. 3:5; 2 Sam. 12:14–18, 24–25). That name from God was the same root as "David," so the prophetic statement implied God's favor and Solomon's succession to the throne.[5] Nathan lived to see that come to pass and make sure God's will for David's successor was honored.

GOD'S HOUSE

As they'd entered the Promised Land, Joshua had told people that God had given them rest and their land of promise (see Josh. 22:4). David finished conquering the land like Joshua had started, and then God gave rest from his enemies. By the Lord's "favor [God had] made [David's] mountain stand strong" (Ps. 30:7). He told Solomon the same thing as Joshua said: "Is not the LORD your God with you? And has He not given you rest on every side?" (1 Chron. 22:18). David had built a house for him and his family. Psalm

30 was written at the house's dedication. However, David told Nathan he was dwelling in a house of cedar while God's presence, the ark, was inside a tent. He wanted to build Him a house. Initially, Nathan said to proceed. However, he spoke that from his opinion, not as God's mouthpiece. How often do we pronounce logic instead of God's words? When that happens, we should react like Nathan, who willingly corrected his error. When the Lord told Nathan to amend what he'd said, he delivered God's message to David as God had said it. Though the Lord was pleased that David wanted to build Him a house (see 2 Sam. 7:2; 1 Kings 8:18), God told David, "You shall not build Me a house to dwell in" (1 Chron. 17:4). Like David, our *perfect* destinies won't always happen because of poor choices we've made along the way.

Beware: *Of those in the prophetic who speak their words, not God's.*

Sometimes God's answer to our deepest heart's desires is simply, "No!" Though His promises are always yes (see 2 Cor. 1:20), He tells us "No!" for many reasons—protection, direction, asking "amiss" (James 4:3). Perhaps He has another plan like He did for building His temple. Nathan asked David if he would build a house for God to dwell in when He hadn't dwelt in a house but in a tent or tabernacle since His children left Egypt. In all that time, He'd never asked anyone to build Him a house of cedar. God's plans were for a tabernacle that wasn't man-made (see Heb. 8:2). He'd taken David from watching sheep to being Israel's king and been with him all along. He cut off his enemies and made him great like other remarkable men on earth. David had rest from the wicked who had oppressed Israel since before the judges' time (see 2 Sam. 7:1, 6–9).

Beware: *Of your reaction when God's answer is "No."*

After David died, the Lord would set up one of his sons to build God's house, and He'd establish that son's kingdom forever, a prophecy about Jesus. If David's son erred, God would chasten him but wouldn't take His mercy away like He had from Saul. In essence, God said, "David, you won't built *Me* a house. I will make *you* a house" (2 Sam. 7:11). God wasn't interested in a building but inhabiting a house—His people. No matter how grand our plans, God's purpose is greater (see 2 Sam. 7:11–16). During our years on earth, we build many things—houses, careers, ministries, families, our own temples. Solomon learned from his dad that nothing prospers if God's not in charge of everything. He penned, "Unless the LORD builds the house, they labor in vain who build it" (Ps. 127:1). God's house would be built, but He wanted it done His way.

Beware: *Of your desire to proceed without God's direction.*

CONCLUSION

David said, "Bless the LORD, all you His hosts, you ministers of His, who do His pleasure!" (Ps. 103:21). Samuel was an important part of David's early years. Nathan was with David since before Solomon was born and was still significant as David was dying. He ensured God's and the king's choice of successor wasn't ignored as another prepared to reign. Solomon was ordained, so God's and David's choice was established. Advisers are crucial for warfare and destiny journeys.

DAVID'S WEAPONS: GOD'S WORD AND TRUST

DAVID'S REFLECTIONS

You number my wanderings; put my tears into Your bottle; are they not in Your book? When I cry out to You, then my enemies will turn back; this I know, because God is for me. In God (I will praise His word), in the LORD (I will praise His word), in God I have put my trust; I will not be afraid. What can man do to me? (Ps. 56:8–11)

GOD'S WORD

I love the lyrics of an old song:
Through it all, through it all,
I've learned to trust in Jesus,
I've learned to trust in God.
Through it all, through it all,
I've learned to depend upon His Word.[1]

This song lists two of David's weapons that can carry us through our journey—God's Word and trust. In Scripture, the Word is many things. As a sword, "the word of God is living and powerful, and sharper than any two-edged sword, piercing even to the division of soul and spirit, and of joints and marrow, and is a discerner of the thoughts and intents of the heart" (Heb. 4:12). This familiar scripture touts the Word's mighty power. This use of "word" is *logos*, God's written Word.[2] It cuts through enemy attacks— sickness, persecution, lies. It's mightier than Saul's and Goliath's great swords, but it can discern minute differences between thoughts and actual intentions. We must get the Word into us during each phase of our journey.

I discussed *rhemas*, a now word, in my "Holy Spirit" section. The written Word, the *logos*, is God's inspired Word that shows truth to bring correction, instruction, and equipping (see 2 Tim. 3:16–17). It's the yardstick by which we measure everything. During our journeys, if something or someone doesn't align with the *logos*, what's being said or done is wrong! Both *logos* and *rhemas* are more powerful weapons than man can devise and send the enemy running because they're forever established in heaven. Jesus is the Word, and He spoke and did only what the Father said and did (see John 1:14; 8:28). When Jesus was in the wilderness before beginning His earthly ministry, satan sought to tempt Him by twisting the Word. Jesus, however, knew to wield God's true Word as a weapon, so He warred with it. He said, "Man shall not live by bread alone, but by every word [*rhema*] that proceeds from the mouth of God" (Matt. 4:4). The enemy understands the Word's power.

After Jesus battled using the Word, satan departed, but that didn't mean Jesus' trials were over. The devil left "until an opportune time" (Luke 4:13). In other words, he'll attack again when it's convenient for him, not us. Especially when we're weakened, he's awaiting occasions to assault and accomplish negative reactions—discouragement, distraction, desertion. Therefore, we should rely on and be familiar with God's Word before going to war. Jesus endured frequent attacks during His three-and-a-half-year ministry, but His foundation in God's flawless, powerful, true Word combatted massive enemy onslaughts. Jesus relied on both the written and spoken word, and so should we because the Father's word sustains us.

Beware: *Of those who twist God's Word.*

OUR WORDS

Isaiah said, "My words which I have put in your mouth, shall not depart from your mouth, nor from the mouth of your descendants... [or] your descendants' descendants...from this time and forevermore" (Isa. 59:21). Promises are sure for us and our posterity. That includes words about destiny. Those promises should be spoken as faith, despite what we perceive in the natural. Words are important, even idle, non-working words. David's son said we can speak life or death with our mouth (see Matt. 12:36; Prov. 18:21). By proclaiming God's word rather than the enemy's threats, we prevail. Our tongues demonstrate what's in our hearts, including faith or fear (see Luke 6:45). Our tongue is one of our most powerful weapons and can be used for blessing, devastation, encouragement, or hurt.

When satan attacks through others' words, we can alter the battle with God's word. Because of His arsenal, "no weapon formed against [us] shall prosper, and every tongue which rises against [us] in judgment [God] shall condemn" (Isa. 54:17). Attacks will come, sometimes as words spoken against us, but they can't succeed. David once said, "All day they twist my words; all their thoughts are against me for evil" (Ps. 56:5). He isn't the only biblical saint who dealt with these dynamics. Verbal attacks intended to damage prophetic integrity happen to God's generals. Once, people who disliked Jeremiah's prophecies plotted to attack him with their tongues and disregard his prophetic words (see Jer. 18:18). Bad mouthing, lying, gossiping—all are enemy-initiated and destructive to us and God's kingdom. However, though others' words can be weapons against us, God's word allows us to stand because He makes our "mouth like a sharp sword… and…a polished shaft; in His quiver He has hidden Me" (Isa. 49:2). God's word spoken through our mouths is a wonderful weapon in our quiver. When we talk on our own, not so much.

Understanding the power of God's words is crucial to a successful destiny journey. As overcomers, His Word should be our obsession and in our "heart[s] like a burning fire shut up in [our] bones" (Jer. 20:9). Regularly being in God's fiery Word allows us to know His promises are sure (see 2 Cor. 1:20). We read, understand, and appropriate God's guarantees then experience their results. When obstacles come, we claim that word as our *rhema*, stand on it, and remember His past faithfulness. God is bound to perform His word because though everything else—even Heaven and earth—doesn't last, His words survive forever (see Matt. 24:35).

If we meditate continually on God's law, His word (see Ps. 1:2), we won't go by what we feel or hear but by what His word says. When we believe and speak the Word rather than enemy pronouncements, victory must come. Keeping it in our minds and hearts and knowing God's faithfulness allows us to claim promises. In Scripture, honey often represents God's word (see Ps. 119:103). Jonathan ate honey and was refreshed. The Lord's sweet, refreshing word supersedes man's reports, threats, or attacks. We're washed by the word (see 1 Sam. 14:27; Eph. 5:26), creating a victor's mindset. David took God at His word, cherished it, and passed his love for and trust in it to his successor. He received and believed promises that transpired for him and his children. The fruition of this was when Jesus was born in his lineage.

When God spoke to David and then to his son, they knew His word was sure. Solomon spoke these words when dedicating the temple:

> You have kept what You promised Your servant David my father; You have both spoken with Your mouth and fulfilled it with Your hand...Lord God of Israel, now keep what You promised Your servant David my father, saying, 'You shall not fail to have a man sit before Me on the throne of Israel, only if your sons take heed to their way, that they walk in My law as you have walked before Me.' (2 Chron. 6:15–17)

TRUST

David said that when he's afraid, he trusts in God (see Ps. 56:3). The opposite of faith and trust is fear. Solomon understood, "The fear of man brings a snare, but whoever trusts in the Lord shall be safe" (Prov. 29:25). Trust is a choice, and confidence develops by experiencing another's faithfulness. Trusting God is better than trusting man or princes (see Ps. 146:3). Though enemies assailed, David knew he could trust the Father to direct his steps and be his shelter no matter the trial nor how bleak its outlook (see Ps. 143:8–9). That attitude comes through experiencing God's faithfulness. You'll be delivered and not defeated if you put your trust in the Lord (see Jer. 39:18). Perhaps that's why David felt conviction after he numbered the people and demonstrated trust in Israel's numbers rather than Israel's God (see 2 Sam. 24). When David heard Goliath's taunts, he was livid that the Philistine without covenant would attack God's people. David knew the Lord would, "let [him] not be ashamed, for [he] put [his] trust in [Him]" (Ps. 25:20). Others thought they had rights that belonged only to God's people. Egyptians assumed they could walk across on dry ground, and Philistines thought they were entitled to the ark (see Exod. 14:23; 1 Sam. 4:17). It ended badly for both. David often acknowledged his persecution but also his trust. Standing steadfast is knowing that no matter what happens, God's mercy surrounds those with covenant who trust in Him (see Ps. 32:10).

Unlike some of David's other sons, Solomon had been born when David was king of all Israel. He must've watched his dad battle various enemies, so he knew David's trust in God was the answer to all issues. He probably witnessed him repeatedly taking petitions to the Father. Solomon said, "Trust in the LORD with all your heart, and lean not on your own understanding; in all your ways acknowledge Him, and He shall direct your paths" (Prov. 3:5–6). Trust Him fully, don't rely on *your* logic, acknowledge Him by your actions, and He'll lead. That's wisdom from a wise man! When we walk by faith, we understand our eye can trick us (see 2 Cor. 5:7).

Though faced with difficult decisions, overwhelming trials, or hurtful betrayals, we should still "rest in the Lord, and wait patiently for Him" (Ps. 37:7). Although David acted out of fear several times during his journey, he ultimately learned to give everything to the Lord. During his Goliath encounter, he demonstrated faith (trust) principles—believing, speaking, acting. He believed implicitly in His God, spoke that to his countrymen and Goliath, then showed trust by acting. He boldly approached the giant with God's choice of weapons. At Ziklag, David knew that though he and his men grieved their losses, the answer was to go to God, so they got back more than they'd lost. When he was dying, he still said God "has redeemed my life from every distress" (1 Kings 1:29). He could pass in peace knowing God had been and would be true to His word. Trust sustained him, even until his death.

Samuel called God "the Strength of Israel" (1 Sam. 15:29). One meaning of that phrase is "trust."[3] Not for just David, but trust was a common trait for God's other generals. Noah, Daniel, the Three Hebrew Children, Moses, Paul—all trusted God despite circumstances. When David performed shepherding duties or escaped from pursuers, Elijah endured drought and persecution, or Joseph spent time in prison, they trusted. Although Joseph's brothers treated him badly, he could later say, "You meant evil against me; but God meant it for good, in order to bring it about as it is this day, to save many people alive" (see Gen. 50:20). That's trust. Though all probably grew weary, they entrusted outcomes to God. Mountains and valleys of destiny journeys nurture trust.

PRAYER

Prayer, one of David's and others' highly tested weapons, also builds trust. Jesus needed prayer time with His Father so much that He often slipped away to find rest, rejuvenation, and communion with Him. Prayer changes things—rain during droughts, escape from pursuing enemies, wisdom for leading others into the Promised Land. Samuel was a prayer warrior. When people said they wanted a king, he was displeased but didn't respond with anger, just prayer (see 1 Sam. 8:6). David also learned to take requests to God for guidance, help, battle plans, his children, repentance. However, he often prayed just because he wanted to exalt the Father. After Nathan gave him the word concerning his covenant with God, David rejoiced and "found it in his heart to pray [a] prayer" of thanksgiving (2 Sam. 7:27).

David prayed twice before battling Philistines in Baal Perazim and Keilah. Then he prayed to see if Keilah's men would deliver him to Saul (see 1 Sam. 23:2–4, 11). When God's answer wasn't what he wanted, he still prayed. After God told Nathan that David's infant son would die, David prayed and fasted all night. When Ahithophel sided with Absalom, David prayed that his counsel would be considered foolishness. Because he approached God often, David knew prayer brought forgiveness and reprimands after he made poor choices. He trusted His wisdom when Shimei assailed him (see 2 Sam. 12:16; 15:31). Even when the Lord was displeased, David knew, "His anger is but for a moment, His favor is for life; weeping may endure for a night, but joy comes in the morning" (Ps. 30:5). Prayer brought success, peace, and victories in David's life.

Prayer is especially effective when we pray for enemies. That's hard when someone constantly belittles and harasses. Despite and because of this, they especially need our love and prayers. Jesus said to, "Love your enemies, do good to those who hate you, bless those who curse you, and pray for those who spitefully use you" (Luke 6:27–28). The Lord restored Job's losses after he prayed for unfaithful friends. When Abraham prayed for Abimelech and his household, fertility returned to his wives. Then, in the next chapter, Sarah conceived after twenty-five years awaiting her Isaac (see Job 42:10; Gen. 20:17–18; 21:2). Praying for enemies isn't what our nature desires, but it's what God expects. Then, Heaven's floodgates open wide, David didn't dwell on others' attacks or consider their superiority but glorified God as he trusted His covenant promises.

CONCLUSION

David said to "taste and see that the Lord is good; blessed is the man who trusts in Him!" (Ps. 34:8). We can trust because His word doesn't return empty but accomplishes what it was sent to perform (see Isa. 55:11). Peter quoted Isaiah that grass and flowers may pass away, but not God's word (see Isa. 40:8; 1 Pet. 1:24–25). David's time with the Father showed him God's faithfulness that developed trust in Him. We discover that, too, with each destiny experience where we "feed on His faithfulness" (Ps. 37:3).

QUESTIONS TO PONDER
(Answers in Appendix)
SIGNIFICANT PROPHETS

1. Give similarities between Samuel and David.

2. Why was Israel's desire for a king a bad thing?

3. How did staying away from battle negatively influence David?

4. Explain how sin trapped David and will entrap us, too.

5. How did Nathan demonstrate the importance of speaking only God's words?

GOD'S WORD and TRUST

6. Explain Hebrews 4:12.

7. How's the Word our yardstick?

8. How can our tongue bring blessings and curses?

9. Show how David trusted even when God punished him.

10. Give examples of what happened when biblical saints prayed for enemies.

Something to Consider: How do David's friends/weapons in this chapter speak about friends/weapons in our lives?

Chapter Eight

MISCELLANEOUS ENEMIES AND FRIENDS

DAVID'S REFLECTIONS

I will be glad and rejoice in You; I will sing praise to Your name.... When my enemies turn back, they shall fall and perish at Your presence. For You have maintained my right and my cause; You sat on the throne judging in righteousness. You have rebuked the nations, You have destroyed the wicked; You have blotted out their name forever and ever. (Ps. 9:2–5)

MISCELLANEOUS ENEMIES

AMALEKITES

Because God has our backs, some challenging enemies play only minor but persistent roles in our lives. When the children in the wilderness headed toward their promised destiny, the Amalekites caused problems for many years. They fought with Israel from the days of Moses to the reign of David (see Exod. 17:8; 1 Sam. 30). Balaam said, "Amalek was first among the nations, but shall be last until he perishes" (Num. 24:20). This statement about being the first refers either to their age or that they first attacked the young nation of Israel. Amalek, Esau's grandson, means "people that licks up."[1] This describes their warfare against the Hebrews. When Israel left one wilderness encampment en route to the next, Amalekites attacked stragglers and weaker travelers who lagged behind that enormous group (see Deut. 25:17–19). Samuel told Saul that God would punish Amalek for what they "did to Israel, how [they] ambushed [them] on the way when [they] came up from Egypt" (see 1 Sam. 15:2). That Amalekite spirit still pursues weaker ones in today's world and church.

Beware: *Of those who prey on the vulnerable.*

They first waged war against Israel when the Hebrews were looking for an oasis, probably during a drought. They attacked at Rephidim and were defeated when Aaron and Hur held up Moses' hands to ensure Joshua's victory. After that, God declared they were an object of perpetual warfare (see Exod. 17:8–13). He said He'd "blot out" their remembrance and that He would "war with Amalek from generation to generation" (Exod. 17:14, 16). After rebelling against God, Israel was defeated by the Amalekites and Canaanites while entering Canaan. They attacked Israel during the judges' (Ehud's and Gideon's) time. King Saul performed systematic harassments against them and other armies (see Num. 14:45; Judg. 3:13; 6:3; 1 Sam. 14:47–48).

Beware: *Of those who cause perpetual warfare.*

Once, against the Amalekites, God told Saul to attack and utterly destroy man, woman, infant, nursing children, oxen, sheep, camels, and donkeys. Saul's massive army—200,000 foot soldiers and 10,000 men of Judah—waited in the valley. Because of their kindness to Israel after leaving Egypt, Saul sent away the Kenites, who were related to Moses by marriage. He attacked and defeated the Amalekites but didn't destroy everything from the plunder. Because he didn't exterminate them as he was told, they continued to raid settlements during his reign (see Judg.

1:16; 1 Sam. 15:1–9). His inability to deal with the Amalekites God's way caused Saul ultimately to lose the kingdom and opened the way to David's destiny.

Beware: *Of consequences for disobedience.*

ZIKLAG

War with the Amalekites happened not only during Saul's reign but also for David. When David and his men returned to Ziklag, Amalekites had attacked and routed their camp. David asked God about pursuing. He said to go and promised victory. They encountered an Egyptian who'd been an Amalekite servant left behind. This was a God encounter. He confirmed they'd burned Ziklag and said he'd show David and his men the Amalekites' camp if they didn't kill him or turn him over to his master. When he led them there, Amalekites were celebrating the enormous spoil they'd seized. However, the enemy's celebration of victory over God's anointed would be short-lived. David attacked constantly for about twenty-four hours, killed all but 400 young men who fled on camels, and retrieved more plunder than the Amalekites had taken. They rescued their families and took flocks and livestock as spoil (see 1 Sam. 30:1, 7–20). This seemingly devastating event turned around to signal a wonderful destiny change for David and his men.

Beware: *Of enemies who take advantage of inattention to plunder you.*

David returned to the 200 men who'd stayed at the Brook Besor because they couldn't go with him. They were probably tired because of the journey from Aphek to Ziklag, about eighty miles.[2] Leaving them there was wise. We should be selective about whom we take into battle or align with in our destiny journeys because others' issues may sway outcomes (see Deut. 20:5-8). When some who had gone with David objected to giving spoil to those who hadn't, David said God had given them victory, so they'd all share. He also sent spoil to Judah's elders who'd helped him (see 1 Sam. 30:21–26). His sharing showed David's love for his people, garnered goodwill with elders, and acknowledged Judah's past losses to the Amalekites.

Beware: *Of those who don't empathize with others' limitations.*

After David returned, he stayed at Ziklag two days. Then, an Amalekite, dirty and wearing torn clothes, arrived from Saul's camp. He fell in front of David and told him he'd escaped from the Israelite camp. He said many had fled from battle and that Saul and his sons were dead. Because David had been busy with the Amalekites and away from the Hebrews and Philistines, he hadn't heard of their deaths. When he asked how the Amalekite knew, he said he happened upon Saul, leaning on his spear but still alive. Saul asked the Amalekite to finish the death, so he complied as an act of kindness. He'd brought Saul's crown and bracelet for David. After David heard this account, he grieved all day. Then he ordered the Amalekite's death because he'd killed God's anointed, even at Saul's dying request (see 2 Sam. 1:1–16). David understood God's command: "Do not touch My anointed ones, and do My prophets no harm" (Ps. 105:15). Keeping correct priorities even against those who have hurt us will serve us well during our journey.

Beware: *Of those who try to gain leadership's favor by assaulting God's anointed.*

SYRIANS AND AMMONITES

The Syrians and Ammonites represent persistent foes who ally with other enemies to hurt our effectiveness. They were first mentioned in the judges' time when Israel served gods of other nations, including Syria (see Judg. 10:6). After David defeated the Philistines and Moabites, he conquered Hadadezer, a Syrian ally and king. David gained great spoil and hamstrung chariot horses except enough for 100 chariots. When Syrians approached to help Hadadezer, David killed 22,000 Syrians. He made garrisons in Syria; they became his servants and brought tribute, including gold shields and bronze. He garnered a name for himself after killing 18,000 Syrians in the Valley of Salt. The Lord preserved him everywhere (see 2 Sam. 8:1–8, 13–14).

Beware: *Of enemies' allies who will spring to their defense.*

When David declared war on Ammon because of their treatment of his servants, they hired many men from Syria, Maacah, and Ish-Tob. Ammon stayed at the city wall while Syrians and others went into the field. Observing their formation, Joab put some of his best men against the Syrians and assigned the remainder under Abishai's command. When Joab and his people drew near, Syrians fled. After the Ammonites saw this, they also ran. When Syrians perceived defeat, they allied with Hadadezer and other Syrians from beyond the river. David brought Israel to fight against Shobach, Hadadezer's commander. The Syrians sustained huge losses, including Shobach. When Hadadezer's kings saw that David had defeated them, they made peace and became his servants. Syrians were afraid to help Ammon anymore (see 2 Sam. 10:6–10, 13–19).

Beware: *Of those who disappear but are actually regrouping for another attack.*

The Ammonites represent an enemy with whom we have a connection from the past but who has chosen to walk in the way of evil. The meaning of Ammon, "the son of my people,"[3] speaks of God's love for them. Though Israel's recurring enemy, the nation began because of Lot's incestuous relationship with his daughter (see Gen. 19:38). Despite these sordid beginnings, God demonstrated how much He loved Lot. During the wilderness journey, Ammonite King Sihon wouldn't let Hebrews pass through his land. Although Israel drove Sihon to Ammon's border, God told Moses not to take Ammonite land because it belonged to Lot's descendants. During the judges' time, Ammon allied with Moab and Amalek and defeated Israel (see Num. 21:23–24; Deut. 2:19; Judg. 3:13).

These nations were also a problem during both Saul's and David's time. The Moabites' connection with Ammon had been an earlier challenge. People from Moab had seduced Israel to commit idolatry and perform sexual acts with Moab's women. In addition, no Ammonite or Moabite could come into God's assembly because they'd hired Balaam to curse them and hadn't brought bread to Israel in the wilderness. When the Ammonites wanted covenant but included the stipulation of the extraction of Israel's citizens' right eyes, Saul responded with anger and soundly defeated them (see Num. 25:1–2; Deut. 23:3–4; 1 Sam. 11:2, 11).

Ammonites again fought Israel when Joab took the army, warred against Rabbah of Ammon, and overthrew the royal city. Joab sent word to David that he'd acquired the water supply for that city. Then, he showed his care for David's legacy and told the king to gather his men and conquer the city lest it be called by Joab's name rather than David's. The king fought at Rabbah and took abundant spoil, including the king's crown with precious stones, weighing a talent of gold, about seventy-five pounds.[4] He made Ammonite people work with bricks, saws, iron picks, and axes (see 2 Sam. 12:26–31).

NABAL

Nabal represents mean-spirited enemies who feel no gratitude for others' kindness. David's encounter with him demonstrates how hasty actions affect destiny. He was briefly in David's life, but his story involved the future king. From Caleb's lineage, Nabal means "fool, senseless,"[5] and that describes his character. After Samuel died, David escaped to the Wilderness of Paran, probably because Saul would be more ruthless without Samuel to buffer. When the wealthy Nabal was shearing sheep nearby, David sent ten men to greet him. They were to speak peace then say they'd heard his shearers were there, so they'd stayed near his shepherds while they were caring for his sheep. David told Nabal to verify with the shepherds about how they'd helped them, and no one had stolen sheep or hurt the men or flock. He asked permission to join them on feast day and for Nabal to provide food. Actually, this wasn't an unreasonable request because masters commonly showed hospitality during sheep-shearing time.[6] David's men approached Nabal with these words (see 1 Sam. 25:1–9).

Beware: *Of expecting those who are harsh or evil to show kindness or gratitude.*

When Nabal heard this message, he was probably already celebrating their sheep-shearing and well on his way to being drunk. He informed David's men that their leader was a nobody he didn't know. Chances are that Nabal *had* heard of David because his wife had. However, he was implying David had no significance and was a servant who left his master. He'd give him no food. When they returned with Nabal's response, David grew angry at this great insult. He told his men to put on swords, and he donned his. He took 400 and left 200 behind to guard supplies (see 1 Sam. 25:10–13). This impetuous response demonstrated an earlier trait in David's character which God refined before he reigned. No record says David sought God before rising against Nabal. As we prepare for battle, God gives direction for how to proceed. Acting impetuously rather than at God's direction isn't the Lord's battle plan and can be devastating to destiny goals.

Beware: *Of rash choices.*

ABIGAIL'S INTERVENTION

God provided guidance through Nabal's wife, Abigail. Though he was "harsh and evil," she was beautiful, with "good understanding" (1 Sam. 25:3). Throughout this scenario with David, she showed wisdom, character, graciousness, and godliness. A servant told Abigail how Nabal had refused David. He confirmed that while they were watching the sheep, David *had* accompanied and protected them from hurt and theft like a wall day and night. Now, he was planning to harm Nabal and his household. The servant asked Abigail to intervene because Nabal was "such a scoundrel that one cannot speak to him" (1 Sam. 25:17). Abigail wisely didn't tell Nabal but sent servants ahead while she quickly gathered massive food and wine for David and his men. Food was already plentiful in preparation for their feast (see 1 Sam. 25:14–19).

Beware: *Of hesitating when you have the ability to circumvent a catastrophe.*

Laden with supplies, she made her way to David and his men. When she met them, David told her that although he'd protected Nabal's possessions, Nabal had repaid his generosity with evil. He vowed to kill all males who belonged to him that night. She quickly got down from her donkey and fell on her face. Humbly at his feet, she told him not to "regard this scoundrel Nabal. For as his name is, so is he: Nabal is his name, and folly is with him!" (1 Sam. 25:25). She said to let Nabal's error fall on her for not having seen David's messengers. She then spoke a prophetic word that the Lord had kept David from seeking vengeance against Nabal and prayed that

David's enemies would be like her husband. She said God had made him an "enduring house" (1 Sam. 25:28) because he fought the Lord's battles, and his heart was pure before Him. She said although a man (Saul) had arisen to kill him, "the life of my lord shall be bound in the bundle of the living with the Lord your God" (1 Sam. 25:29). She told him God would sling his enemies away (see 1 Sam. 25:20–29). This probably resonated with David, former sheep-protector and giant-slayer with a sling. God guards His treasures by putting them in a protected place, tying them up, then catapulting enemies away.

Beware: *Of not allowing God to resolve a thing.*

ACTING HASTILY

Revenge belongs to God, not us. Moses declared that the Lord curses those who hate and persecute us (see Deut. 30:7). Abigail said she knew he was anointed and to remember her when he became king. She cautioned him to act judiciously, for killing Nabal could change his destiny. David was touched by her words and reacted in humility, not anger or vengeance. He praised God for sending Abigail, accepted her gifts and, thanked her for advice that kept him from bloodshed by his hand. He then sent her home in peace. By taking a chance on David's wisdom and fairness she saved her household and kept David from making a grave mistake. When she returned, Nabal was feasting and very drunk. She waited until morning after he sobered up to tell him she'd taken supplies to David. He became so angry he had a stroke or heart attack and died about ten days later. When David heard of Nabal's death, he acknowledged God's hand and again praised the Lord for keeping him from acting in vengeance (see 1 Sam. 25:31–39). Through this experience David grew toward his kingship destiny as he allowed God to determine his and his enemies' fates.

Beware: *Of consequences for rejecting God's anointed.*

David learned much about God's retribution and later commented not to seek one's own retribution because evil doers will be cut down by God (see Ps. 37:2). He understood that those who come against God's anointed pay a price. When he had a second chance to kill Saul, David told Abishai that the Lord will "return... [the enemies'] wickedness...on [their] own head[s]" (1 Sam. 25:39). David knew God would "contend with him who contends with you, and...will save your children" (Isa. 49:25). The last part of that promise literally happened. David sent servants to propose to Abigail. She humbly submitted herself as his servant, rose quickly, took five maidens, rode on a donkey, followed his messengers, and became his wife. She bore Chileab (also called Daniel), David's second son (see 1 Sam. 25:39–42; 2 Sam. 3:3; 1 Chron. 3:1). Abigail's actions protected David's destiny but also brought her into her own.

MISCELLANEOUS FRIENDS

DAVID'S REFLECTIONS

A posterity shall serve Him. It will be recounted of the Lord to the next generation, they will come and declare His righteousness to a people who will be born, that He has done this. (Ps. 22:30–31)

SOLOMON

Some friends who help us in our destiny journeys perform major roles while the Lord sends others for a season. As David's son and successor, Solomon represents those for whom we have responsibility to train to continue our legacy. David said, "One generation shall praise Your works to another, and shall declare Your mighty acts" (Ps. 145:4). Solomon did that. He was David's son but mentioned only briefly during David's life. Unlike most of his sons, he was faithful to David. Like his father, he was God's choice despite others better positioned and qualified to reign. As David was dying, he told Solomon to be strong and prove himself; observe God's charge; walk in His ways; and keep His statutes, commandments, judgments, and testimonies. He reminded him of God's promise that if David's sons kept God's truths, they'd always be over Israel's throne. David gave Solomon instructions for after his death, and Solomon fulfilled them (see 1 Kings 2:1–4).

Despite his creating a tabernacle, David wanted to honor God by building a temple. However, the Lord said that after David's death, Solomon would be chosen because he wouldn't be a man of war. God would "give him rest from all his enemies all around" (1 Chron. 22:9). David praised God and asked Him to establish His promise so God's name would be magnified forever. While David was ruling and Solomon was about eighteen,[7] he gave his son temple plans, priests' duties, workmen, trees, and precious metals. David commanded that foreigners be gathered in Israel and for masons to cut hewn stone to build God's house. As a young man, Solomon was likely overwhelmed with the building project's enormity, so David went even further. Because he wanted the Lord's house to be wonderful, he helped Solomon gather other materials and ordered leaders to help his son. He even donated from his treasury (see 1 Chron. 17:23; 22:2-5, 17; 28:1–4; 29:3). If God's our priority, we give generously and work diligently.

David warned Solomon to seek God's commandments so he could possess the good land to leave for his children. He told him to "know the God of your father" (1 Chron. 28:9). That word *know* is used infrequently in older scriptures. It deals with seeking relationship with the Father.[8] David, who loved God's presence, wanted his son also to desire relationship with the Lord! He told Solomon to serve Him with a loyal heart and willing mind and reminded him that God searches hearts and understands intents or thoughts. He told his son to seek Him; if he forsook the Lord, He'd cast him off forever (see 1 Chron. 28:9).

As God molded Solomon into the mighty king he'd become, He gave wisdom about ruling. After the temple's dedication, the Lord appeared to him at night and said, "If My people who are called by My name will humble themselves, and pray and seek My face, and turn from their wicked ways, then I will hear from heaven, and will forgive their sin and heal their land" (2 Chron. 7:14). Israel forgot that admonition often, and so did Solomon. Although he was wise and reigned in peace, at the end of his days, he was influenced by his numerous, heathen wives and followed other gods. This wise man should've heeded his own words: "He who walks with wise men will be wise, but the companion of fools will be destroyed" (Prov. 13:20).

God punished Solomon by taking away most of the kingdom from his son, but He demonstrated love for David by delaying Solomon's judgment then allowing the family to retain part of the kingdom. His choices were more like Saul's than David's—they lost all or part of their kingdom and persecuted God's selection for their replacements (see 1 Kings 11:4, 11–12; 12:20; 11:40). No matter how well we've lived, righteousness and obedience have no expiration date. They both determine destiny for us and others.

BEWARE: *Of those who have a lifetime of good yet don't finish well.*

DAVID'S MIGHTY MEN

David's mighty men of valor were an impressive force for the kingdom and a necessity during David's destiny journey. They represented strength in unity. Christians have a destiny—to be part of the army that fights for the King. We aren't an army of one but need loyal, anointed people to assist and defend us in *our* callings, through *their* callings. The first mention of David's group who became his mighty men was in Adullam. As evidence of his leadership skills, he took those defeated men then organized them into powerful warriors. His crew of 400 misfits grew to be his band of 600 mighty men whose feats helped him become Israel's greatest king. These men faithfully served him through his many struggles and supported his choice of successor as he was dying (see 1 Kings 1:8). When David spoke his last words, he highlighted accomplishments of thirty-seven men he honored and acknowledged their great victories.

BEWARE: *Of neglecting to mentor others into mighty men and women of God.*

One man killed 800 men at one time. Another attacked Philistines until his hand became weary and stuck to his sword. Another stood in the middle of a lentil field and killed Philistines. Once, when they were fighting near where David grew up, he remembered and craved the sweet coolness of Bethlehem's wells. Three mighty men broke through to get it. Another man killed 300 with his spear, and one killed two fierce Moabites and a lion in a pit on a snowy day. Bathsheba's father and husband were mighty men with skill and integrity. How fitting that among those with superior abilities, Uriah was listed last in the place of honor (see 2 Sam. 23:8–39). He also received acknowledgement in the New Testament. While enumerating Jesus' genealogy, one entry says, "David the king begot Solomon by her who had been the wife of Uriah" (Matt. 1:6). God doesn't forget the spilled blood of those who die innocently and with integrity. The destinies of all these men provide a lesson. David may have been king, but his men's callings were important, too, in his destiny journey.

OTHERS

In the worst of times, God raises miscellaneous friends to help us realize His plan and reassure us during our journeys. Encouraging others encourages us. Fleeing from Absalom, David met Shobi, son of Nahash from Ammon, and Machir, son of Ammiel from Lo Debar. They brought supplies to David and his people. Machir was probably related to Bathsheba. Her dad was Eliam (Ammiel) (see 2 Sam 11:3; 1 Chron. 3:5), so Machir was likely her brother. Items included beds, basins, earthen vessels, wheat, barley, flour, parched grains and beans, lentils and parched seeds, honey and curds, sheep, and cheese (see 2 Sam. 17:27–29). How these articles must have touched David and his men who were hungry, tired, and discouraged! They surely needed to know people supported David in both their hearts and actions. What a wonder that even in our worst times when we feel like fleeing from the path where He's directed us, God provides, often through others! Jesus spoke of the importance of giving to those working for God's kingdom. When we're faithful to supply their needs, we receive the same reward as they (see Matt. 10:41). Too often we find excuses for why we won't support them, but we're cheating them and ourselves. To reach our destinies, caring for God's leaders is essential.

Beware: *Of those who silently support you but do nothing to help.*

Barzillai, the Gileadite, also helped David and his men. Later, David demonstrated how much that gesture meant. While returning to Jerusalem after Absalom's death, Barzillai, eighty and extremely rich, escorted David across the Jordan. Though David invited him to come to Jerusalem as his guest, Barzillai said he was too old; in his stead, he said Chimham, probably Barzillai's son, would be David's servant. After he crossed over, David kissed and blessed Barzillai, who returned home. Barzillai wasn't seeking wealth or personal time with the king. He could've had anything, but his purpose for helping David wasn't to receive rewards but to love and respect the king. Do we serve our King for what He'll give us or simply because we love Him? As David was dying, he bestowed honor on Barzillai's descendants by telling Solomon to show kindness to his sons and let them eat at his table because of their dad's generosity. Barzillai's sons were also later mentioned in the remnant that repaired Jerusalem's walls (see 2 Sam. 19:31–39; 1 Kings 2:7; Neh. 7:63).

Beware: *Of doing good things because of rewards.*

Many others befriended David at different times. When Toi (Tou in 1 Chron. 18), king of Hamath, heard David had defeated Hadadezer, he sent his son to greet and bless King David with precious metals. Ittai the Gittite, who'd been with David only one day before he fled from Absalom, swore his allegiance and crossed over with David, saying: "In whatever place my lord the king shall be, whether in death or life, even there also your servant will be" (2 Sam. 15:21). When David gathered materials to build his house, friends from other nations contributed with workers and supplies (see 2 Sam. 8:9–10; 15:19–20; 5:11). Friends are an amazing weapon to combat enemies and help us fulfill destiny.

CONCLUSION

David counted on the Lord to keep him "from the hands of the wicked [and] violent men, who have purposed to make [his] steps stumble" (Ps. 140:4). David faced many enemies but cultivated many friendships during his calling season and beyond. Mourning the loss of his king and his friend/brother, he told people to teach their children a song about Saul and Jonathan (see 2 Sam. 1:19–27). Celebrating our enemies as well as friends demonstrates love, even to the unlovable. David's attitude of love and devotion to the Lord, plus David's enemies and friends, provided precious weapons that served him well during each phase of his journey.

DAVID'S WEAPONS: INTEGRITY AND PREPARATION

DAVID'S REFLECTIONS

By this I know that You are well pleased with me, because my enemy does not triumph over me. As for me, You uphold me in my integrity, and set me before Your face forever. (Ps. 41:11–12).

Part of a godly arsenal includes character, which the Lord wants to refine during our destiny journeys. Many who've received callings and are awaiting the move into destiny don't understand the refinement process. For integrity to grow, we must tenaciously pursue God and practice a sold-out, separated life. Actions influence destiny. This psalm speaks of how David arrived at his godly goal. His integrity and preparation served him well for what he'd become:

[God]...chose the tribe of Judah.... He also chose David His servant, and took him from the sheepfolds; from following the ewes that had young He brought him, to shepherd Jacob His people, and Israel His inheritance. So he shepherded them according to the integrity of his heart, and guided them by the skillfulness of his hands. (Ps. 78:68, 70–72)

God was looking for someone who had His heart because His objectives were bigger than just Israel's throne. He wanted someone through whom His Son's lineage could come. When God chose Judah then David, He had more obvious alternatives. Judah had a sketchy history, but God used his line to establish the kingdom. Chosen literally coming from the sheepfolds, David wasn't the best Jesse had to offer, but God had a plan.

INTEGRITY

According to the above passage, God promotes using two criteria: integrity of heart and skillfulness of hands. In this scripture, "integrity" is *tom*, "completeness...upright (-ly, -ness)."[1] In large part, integrity has fallen out of vogue and been replaced by darkness of heart. Even many Christians compromise on everything from taxes to tithes to fidelity. When God picks His army, He considers the heart to measure a person's integrity, not what he or she shows outwardly. Isaiah's words about character are powerful: "The treacherous dealer deals treacherously, and the plunderer plunders" (Isa. 21:2). It's simple: If we deal treacherously with others, we're treacherous. If we plunder, we're a plunderer. If we lie, we're a liar. If we cheat, we're a cheater. We can talk a good game, go to church, show others a façade, but our heart is ultimately revealed. Actions and fruit define us and show hearts and character. Then we're rewarded "according to the fruit of [our] doings" (Jer. 17:10). Integrity matters to God and should to us, too. Godly choices demonstrate godly character.

When God and satan conversed about Job, God described him as a man who "holds fast to his integrity" (Job 2:3). "Holding fast to integrity" describes David, too. Integrity was fashioned in him as a boy and deepened experience-by-experience. When his father told him to take food to his brothers at the front, he obeyed. However, he didn't shirk his duties with the sheep but put them in another's care while he was gone (see 1 Sam. 17:20). That's integrity. He walked "in integrity of heart and in uprightness" (1 Kings 9:4), so God considered him a man of honor though he made many mistakes. After he numbered Israel and caused the plague, David told God that destruction should come against him and his family, not others (see 2 Sam. 24:17). That's integrity. He also grieved and honored Abner after his death. As he followed the coffin, the name, "King David," was first used (see 2 Sam. 3:31). Integrity is necessary to bring us into destiny.

Beware: *Of those whose actions display weak integrity.*

In Ziklag, David's sense of fairness prompted him to give spoil to men who'd been physically unable to go to battle (see 1 Sam. 30:24). He loved his men, even those who hadn't actively participated in the great victory. His actions were a contrast to others who were called "wicked and worthless men" when they didn't want to share spoils (see 1 Sam. 30:22). Another time when his mighty men traveled to get him water, he refused to drink but rather poured it out as a sacrifice to the Lord. He couldn't enjoy it when they'd exposed themselves to potential danger to procure that water. No one was worthy of such a sacrifice except the Lord. That's integrity.

Beware: *Of leaders who put their needs and desires before others'.*

TOWARD SAUL

Among his last words, David commented on fairness in a leader's character: "He who rules over men must be just" (2 Sam. 23:3). Saul didn't practice that as a ruler, especially toward David. David did toward Saul, though, even when he had opportunities to kill him, be finished with Saul's persecution, and claim the throne. David wouldn't harm him; and no matter what Saul did, he didn't "repay...evil for evil" (Rom. 12:17). He was strong and garnered good will because of his character. His integrity was apparent even after Saul's death. Ishbosheth was Saul's fourth and youngest son. He wasn't at the battle with his brothers, so he became king after their deaths. He turned out to be a weak ruler, so he probably hadn't been included in the fatal battle because he was likely an ineffective soldier, too. Civil war erupted during his reign, and Israel suffered much loss at Judah's hands (see 2 Sam. 3:1).

After Abner's murder, Ishbosheth grew disheartened, so the land became even more troubled. Two of Ishbosheth's captains approached him while he lay napping, stabbed him in his stomach, killed, and beheaded him. They took his head to David and said, "Here is the head of Ishbosheth, the son of Saul your enemy, who sought your life; and the LORD has avenged my lord the king this day of Saul and his descendants" (2 Sam. 4:8). David didn't respond with jubilation but rather indignation. This was the leader of God's nation, son of the king whom God had anointed. David had loved and sworn not to cut off his house. He was David's brother-in-law and best friend's brother. Ishbosheth was defenseless when they killed him. Instead of rewarding them, he reminded them how he'd executed the man who claimed to have killed Saul, so why not those who killed Saul's son in his bed? That's integrity. He commanded them to be slain, their hands and feet be cut off, and be hanged in Hebron. He honored Ishbosheth by burying his head with Abner (see 2 Sam. 4:1–2, 5–12). Fairness and integrity defined David and were key to unlocking his destiny. Will your integrity pass the test to allow you to proceed into your destiny?

PREPARATION

The second aspect of David's training for reigning was the "skillfulness of his hands." The word for "skillfulness" is *towbunah*, meaning "intelligence... reason...understanding, wisdom."[2] God fosters those traits in us, but we prepare for our destinies through experience and instruction. We couldn't step into natural vocations—doctors, teachers, architects, mechanics—without education and training. Being diligent counts toward what we'll become. Jesus gave the parable where the master paid his servants differing numbers of talents (5-2-1). Two servants doubled theirs while the third buried his. The master gave more to those who'd been productive (see Matt. 25:14–28). He then called the third a "wicked and lazy servant" (Matt. 25:26). What are we doing to bring wealth to the Master?

Usually an interval ensues between calling and destiny—Joseph, Abraham, Moses, Jesus. During that time it's easy to wonder if God remembers our calling because most of us want promises to happen yesterday. However, rushing into destiny doesn't make us destiny-ready. Samuel anointed both Saul and David as kings of Israel. One was ready; one wasn't. Saul was tapped as king then took office shortly afterward. David had nearly twenty years of preparation. A godly king requires both anointing and preparation before wearing the crown. In the meantime, while we await our call's fruition, we occupy and work. Solomon's instruction has been my mantra: "Whatever your hand finds to do, do it with your might" (Eccles. 9:10). Life, warfare, nor destiny preparation should be haphazard, and each job is important to reaching our goals. When Elijah tapped Elisha to be his successor, he was working with twelve yoke of oxen. Then, before he became Elijah's replacement prophet, he assisted as his servant, learning and getting ready for his double-portion ministry (see 2 Kings 3:11). Staying diligent helps integrity because when we're "not busy [we can become] busybodies"

(2 Thess. 3:11 NIV). Preparation or lack of matters to stepping into that calling or missing what we were born to do. Too many treat their callings with indifference rather than single-minded determination to arrive at the goal. David's preparation shows that while we're awaiting destiny, God's training us for whatever our journey brings.

Beware: *Of those who want to arrive at destiny but not invest necessary preparation.*

THE SHEPHERD'S LOVE

Shepherds teach much about preparing for destiny because "we are the people of His pasture, and the sheep of His hand" (Ps. 95:7). A good shepherd protects and loves his sheep. David was a good shepherd who learned how to love and better guide his sheep by observing the Great Shepherd. He shares insights in Psalm 23. The Shepherd makes His sheep not suffer want. He replenishes their souls with rest and restoration. He shows the way of righteousness (integrity), so He can be glorified. When bad times come, even if death is so close its shadow makes fear try to creep in, we can walk, not run away, because our Shepherd is with us. He guides with His rod and comforts with His staff. He feeds us, even with enemies around. He then anoints us, gives us plenty, and lets His goodness and mercy pursue. Relationship with the Shepherd brings good beyond measure and lets us dwell forever with Him. This consummate Shepherd cares for and about His sheep, and so should we as we prepare to be a good shepherd to various flocks we serve during our journey.

The Shepherd loves His lambs: "He will feed His flock like a shepherd; He will gather the lambs with His arm, and carry them in His bosom, and gently lead those who are with young" (Isa. 40:11). This word for "shepherd" is *raah*, meaning "to tend a flock…companion…make friendship with."[3] That picture describes how the Father loves His lambs. He's not only our Shepherd but our friend and companion. He holds us in His arms and pulls us tightly to His breast. If we're weak, He leads us so our little ones, destinies we may birth, aren't lost. A shepherd gathers his sheep into the sheepfold and uses his body to block the entrance so they don't wander off or be harmed by predators (see Ps. 68:13). Doesn't that sound like God's love as He protects His own?

Jesus also discussed traits of a shepherd. He said a true shepherd "calls his own sheep by name" (John 10:3). Intimacy with the Shepherd shows that He knows our name, and we know His voice. Jesus also said the "good shepherd gives His life for the sheep" (John 10:11). Unfortunately, many who call themselves "shepherds" don't mentor others with the goal of leading and preparing them for destiny. Instead of protecting the flock, their objective is to keep them from leaving to attend another church. My husband calls those ranchers, not shepherds. Jesus called them "hireling[s]" (John 10:12), who run from the wolf because they don't truly care about the sheep (see John 10:13). They lead others for what it will do for *them*—their finances, resume, name. Hirelings may be "savage wolves" (Acts 20:29) in sheep's clothing or so unconcerned about their sheep that the wolf gets in. When that happens, "woe to shepherds who destroy and scatter the sheep" (Jer. 23:1). Part of preparation is observing how a true shepherd interacts with his flock.

Beware: *Of leaders who lack experience, insight, and true love for the people.*

FOR OTHERS

If we love like God does, we use gifts, strengths, and talents to lead others to good pasture. We care for the flock, whether sparse and seemingly insignificant or as grand as God's nation. At first, Saul was considerate of God's laws and others. He wanted to take something to Samuel, God's prophet, as he inquired about his dad's donkeys (see 1 Sam. 9:7). After he became king, his humility waned; he was all about self—his ego, reputation, kingdom, legacy, monument, desires. By contrast, David loved his people and built relationship with them and His Father. Every job was important; and everyone and everything, even his sheep, were, too. Before he became a warrior and king, David the shepherd loved his flock and achieved victories over predators. Those experiences built confidence to confront enemies when he became the nation's shepherd.

We once spoke to a small congregation that met at a YMCA in Arizona. The facilities were adequate except the bathroom often had no paper towels. One lady who drove nearly two hours to attend had a heart for others. She prepared by bringing paper towels, but not still on the roll. She tore them off, folded them perfectly, and laid them on the sink counter in her best basket. What we do for the Lord and others and how we do it makes a difference—watching our animals, shepherding a nation, providing paper towels. Fulfilling our smallest job for God and others correlates with our taking one more step toward destiny.

Much of David's kinghood success began as his flock's shepherd. While a boy, he was miraculously anointed. Then, he experienced a lengthy training season on the way to destiny fulfillment. During those years, he worked diligently on what came into his path to refine his shepherding craft—calming demons, eluding enemies, serving as a leader in Saul's army. His relentless practice with his sling ultimately served him well. In the process, he acquired much knowledge about battles and victory. Because he'd learned during his life, David understood the importance of preparation and took his knowledge into future battles. He was a good shepherd who risked his life for his animals and his human sheep but knew God was his sufficiency. His army prepared for battle the best they could but understood the outcome was the Lord's (see 2 Sam. 10:11–12). When he reigned as king of Judah, several years would pass before he ruled all Israel. He still had much to perfect, but God doesn't waste experiences in our destiny preparation.

PREPARING FOR GOD'S HOUSE

David's preparation didn't stop when he became king. He prepared for Israel's future by naming God's choice for his successor. Israel's leadership history had proven that was important. Despite evil sons, Eli found a successor in the boy he mentored, and Samuel found David. David's older sons also lacked integrity; so his God-chosen successor would be the younger son, Solomon. Before he brought back the ark, he prepared for its arrival by erecting a tent. Later, he planned for the temple's construction (see 1 Chron. 15:1). Though he wasn't allowed to construct it, David didn't abandon that project. God made others "understand in writing, by His hand upon [David], all the works of the plans" for the temple (1 Chron. 28:19).

David prepared when he chose the temple site. When the Lord answered David with fire on the altar (see 1 Chron. 21:26), that great sign may have made David decide that was the location God was consecrating.[4] At that time, the tabernacle was in Gibeon, but David said he couldn't go there to call on God because of the angel's sword. He decided God's altar would be located on Ornan's threshing floor (see 1 Chron. 21:29–30; 22:1). This was a God-ordained decision and part of the preparation to help Solomon. David assembled Israel's leaders at Jerusalem, stood before them, and said he desired to build a house for the ark (see 1 Chron. 28:2). Subsequently, he made "abundant preparations before his death" and took "much trouble to prepare for the house of the LORD" (1 Chron. 22:5, 14). He left instructions, probably told to Gad or Nathan or written down for after his death.[5] Preparation continued as he helped the inexperienced Solomon to make the Lord's house "exceedingly magnificent, famous and glorious throughout all countries" (1 Chron. 22:5).

David helped his son prepare by gathering construction supplies—workers; iron for nails, doors, gates, and joints; plus ample gold, bronze, and cedar. He prayed a prosperity blessing for Solomon and provided plans for each section, materials, and workers. He even prepared for temple maintenance—from spoils Israel had taken and others' contributions to the temple treasury, including Samuel, Saul, Abner, and Joab. Various Israeli leaders gave willingly for the work of God's house—gold, silver, bronze, iron, jewels (see 1 Chron. 26:27–28; 29:4–9). The total he collected in today's amounts would be $1 billion, 800 thousand in gold and $84 million in silver.[6] David's preparation to create an amazing house for God's ark was good for him, Solomon, the Lord's work, and the Lord's nation.

CONCLUSION

David once said, "The Lord rewarded me according to my righteousness; according to the cleanness of my hands He has recompensed me" (Ps. 18:20). The Lord looks at integrity when He hands out assignments, but He also looks at diligence to prepare. I once heard the saying if we fail to prepare, we prepare to fail. Before Elijah ran his amazing race, "he girded up loins" (see 1 Kings 18:46). Jeremiah also said to "gird up thy loins, and arise" (Jer. 1:17 KJV), or "prepare yourself and arise" (NKJV). Too many want opportunities to fall upon them instead of doing whatever they can to prepare for God's assignment. Preparation brings greater things.

QUESTIONS TO PONDER
(Answers in Appendix)
MISCELLANEOUS ENEMIES and FRIENDS

1. What's the main characteristic that made Amalekites devious enemies?

2. Why did David give spoils to men who stayed behind at Ziklag?

3. How did God show His love for Lot?

4. Describe how Nabal's name demonstrates his character.

5. How did Abigail protect David?

6. Why was Solomon included with David's friends?

7. How did David acknowledge his mighty men as he was dying?

8. Whom did he put into the place of honor?

9. How did David demonstrate that Barzillai's kindness touched him deeply?

INTEGRITY and PREPARATION

10. According to Psalm 78:67–72, what are criteria listed for David's success as Israel's shepherd?

11. Explain Isaiah 21:2.

12. Give examples of David's integrity.

13. What's the difference between Saul's and David's preparation to rule?

14. Contrast a good and bad shepherd.

Something to Consider: How do David's enemies/friends/weapons in this chapter speak about our enemies/friends/weapons today?

Part Three

DAVID'S FRIENDS, TURNED ENEMIES

Chapter Nine

JOAB

DAVID'S REFLECTIONS

It is not an enemy who reproaches me; then I could bear it. Nor is it one who hates me who has exalted himself against me; then I could hide from him. But it was you, a man my equal, my companion and my acquaintance. We took sweet counsel together, and walked to the house of God in the throng. (Ps. 55:12–14)

Warfare is inherently sad when friends become enemies. Often this shapes destiny because they not only desert us but work counter-productively to God's purpose for us. Like Saul, who at one time loved David, many friends later betrayed him. Joab represents a great necessity in warfare—a capable general who understands warfare strategy and whom we can trust. That person should love and support us like Joab loved David. Unfortunately, Joab became his enemy as weak character traits emerged. He began as David's go-to person, ardent supporter, nephew, friend, confidant, and general. He watched over David's choices and gave counsel based on protecting David's legacy and others' perceptions. Joab made many good decisions, but other times his actions negatively affected David. He was with David from before he was king to the end of his forty-year reign, but that alliance wasn't always good. Over time, David would regret his dependence on Joab when his faulty integrity affected him and others David loved and respected.

Beware: *Of those with integrity issues that will harm your destiny.*

DAVID'S GENERAL

Joab's leadership role began when David and his men went to Jerusalem against the Jebusites, whose taunts made them "hated by David's soul" (2 Sam. 5:8). They challenged David, saying he was too inept to come there and that he could be beaten by the lame or blind. This was similar to how Goliath taunted the Israelites. Derision is a common enemy ploy to take focus off destiny and victory. David disproved the giant and Jebusites' predictions with an Israeli victory. He said whichever of his men climbed the water shaft to defeat the Jebusites would be his chief and captain. Joab ascended first and became commander (see 2 Sam. 5:6–8; 1 Chron. 11:6–8). While Joab repaired the rest of the city, David built around it and became great because the LORD was with him (see 2 Sam. 5:10). After Ammonites humiliated David's servants, Joab again showed great military skills. He and Abishai led men on two sides against the Syrians. When their enemies saw the Hebrews, they ran. They later fought against Ammon at Rabbah, the same place he'd sent Uriah to the front line. This battle showed Joab's love for David when he wanted the city to bear David's name (see 2 Sam. 10:9–14; 12:26–28). Fulfilling destiny sometimes means promoting others to their leadership roles.

Beware: *Of those whose battle plan is to defeat you through ridicule.*

URIAH'S DEATH

Joab's role in Uriah's death demonstrated negative character. After David had sent his men to war with Ammon at Rabbah, Uriah became dispensable because of his uprightness. Ironically, his refusal to be with his wife was due to his love and devotion for Joab, other warriors, and the king. David didn't see this contradiction but rather used it to commit an atrocity. He wrote a letter to Joab and, in an even more deplorable act, sent it by Uriah's hand. David respected Uriah's honesty not to open the letter. He told Joab to put him in the hottest battle spot so he'd die. When he read it, Joab certainly knew something nefarious was happening, but he complied with David's request. Both these men's actions contrasted with the upstanding Uriah (see 2 Sam. 11:6, 14–15). Obviously, his character exceeded his king's and commander's.

Beware: *Of acting without integrity to keep sin hidden.*

Joab put Uriah with valiant men in battle. He and others of David's mighty men died that day. Joab made sure David didn't blame him and sent word about their great losses and that Uriah was dead. He was complicit in Uriah's death, but his comments seem like a veiled threat to reveal David's actions. Servants told David, and he answered in a hard-hearted way: "The sword devours one as well as another" (2 Sam. 11:25). He said to tell Joab not to be discouraged but rather to defeat them (see 2 Sam. 11:16–25). When we lose sight of God's plan because of our own motivations, everyone involved suffers.

Beware: *Of those who commit an atrocity for you because they'll also commit one against you.*

WITH ABSALOM

Joab's bad character again showed in two incidents involving Absalom. When he was banished after Amnon's death, Joab used trickery to convince David to bring his son back. He surreptitiously told a wise woman to pretend to be mourning for her son. She should go to the king, fall on her face, prostrate herself, and claim to be a widow whose son had killed his brother. The family wanted her to give them the surviving son, so they could slay him in retribution. She said her remaining son's death would erase all that remained of her and her husband (see 2 Sam. 14:1–7). Because her story was a parable about her family's feelings toward her son, it's a good assumption that David's family was against Absalom because of Amnon's murder.

Beware: *Of those who use deception to accomplish their purpose.*

The king told her to go home, and he'd give orders concerning the situation. He promised to protect her, and not a hair on her son's head would be hurt. Then, she asked why he defended her son but wouldn't return his own banished son. She said he'd schemed against God's people by not bringing Absalom home. David's response was to ask if Joab had put her up to this (see 2 Sam. 14:8–19). That question says much. He distrusted his general because Joab had done much and would later do more to show his conniving character. He not only had surreptitiously schemed to bring Absalom back, but he'd later violate David's wishes where Absalom and then Solomon were concerned. He wouldn't number as David had asked because "the king's word was abominable to Joab" (1 Chron. 21:6). Personal destiny is influenced when we lack submission to leadership.

The woman confirmed that Joab had told her what to say. David told him to bring Absalom back but that he must go to his own house and not see David. Joab's helping Absalom's cause ultimately created much pain to David. Two years after Absalom's return, Joab made another error. He talked the king into receiving him, but reconciliation was a mistake for David. It opened the door for Absalom's overthrow attempt (see 2 Sam. 14:19–33). However, the worst of Joab's actions against David was yet to come. During Absalom's insurrection, Joab would drastically violate David's trust and orders. Joab had devolved from a devotee to one without submission.

Beware: *Of continued association with those having duplicitous characters.*

ABSALOM'S DEATH

As David fought to regain the kingdom from Absalom, he put Joab, Abishai, and Ittai each in charge of one third of the army. The king gave an order to "deal gently for my sake with the young man Absalom" (2 Sam. 18:5). Everyone heard this, including Joab. His actions, however, again showed lack of submission. After a great battle, a man told Joab he'd seen Absalom hanging in a tree. When Joab asked why he hadn't killed him, he reminded the general that David had warned everyone, including Joab, not to touch Absalom. He'd have endangered his life with the king, and then Joab would've also turned against him. These statements tell a lot about Joab and how others knew about his questionable integrity. Joab took three spears and stabbed Absalom through the heart. Then ten of his armor bearers surrounded Absalom and killed him. Joab blew the trumpet to call people back (see 2 Sam. 18:1–5, 10–13, 15–16).

Beware: *Of those who incite actions they'll later use against you.*

Several reasons may explain why Joab stabbed Absalom, contrary to his king's orders. He loved David, so he may have been seeking vengeance for Absalom's defiance to the king. He may have been ensuring Absalom wouldn't hurt him again. However, his reason was probably more self-serving. He didn't like Absalom. He resented his bullying to intercede with David then burning his fields. He probably despised Absalom's lack of respect and haughty answers when others showed great deference for Joab's position. Joab may have also still been angry about David's meeting with Abner, his potential rival. Whatever his reason for disobeying the king's command, his actions brought an end to the war Absalom had started but created a great rift between him and David. Joab's destiny had been tied to David's, but his lack of submission and character affected where he could go in his destiny.

Beware: *Of those who ignore leadership's orders.*

When someone told Joab that David was weeping about Absalom, "victory that day was turned into mourning for all the people" (2 Sam. 19:2). Because of David's grief, everyone appeared ashamed, like one who fled from battle. David continued to mourn for Absalom; and Joab seemed supportive, though he'd caused David's pain. He approached David and said followers had saved David and his household. David's extreme grief implied love for his enemies and hatred for his friends. He said David would've been pleased if Absalom had lived, but that meant David and his loyal followers would've died. He urged David to comfort his servants because if he didn't, no one would stay with him after that day. Those results would be worse than anything he'd experienced in his life. David sat at the gate, and everyone approached (see 2 Sam. 19:1–8). However, he certainly didn't forget Joab's responsibility for his son's death.

AMASA

Another event made David regret his association with Joab. It was related to Amasa, son of David's sister Abigail. As David restructured his army after Absalom's rebellion, he made Amasa captain instead of Joab. Then, he dealt with another rebellion—Sheba. David told Amasa to bring Judah's men in three days to fight Sheba. Amasa left to gather them but took longer than David requested. David had shown his mistrust of Joab by appointing Amasa; when Amasa was delayed, he again showed his doubts. He sent Abishai, not Joab, to pursue Sheba before he could get established in a city and escape. Later, the leadership position reverted to Joab, perhaps because Abishai thought his brother would kill him, too, to protect his rank. The group that pursued Sheba met with Amasa at the large stone in Gibeon (see 1 Chron. 2:17; 2 Sam. 19:13; 20:1, 4–8, 23).

As Joab approached Amasa dressed in battle armor, his sword fell out. He asked Amasa if he was well then took him by the beard with his right hand as if to kiss him. Amasa didn't notice the sword in Joab's hand; he stabbed Amasa, whose insides fell out. David would later allude to this slaughter when he talked about Joab's atrocities and that Amasa's blood had literally been on Joab's belt and sandals. Joab may have killed his cousin because he resented Amasa's delay in coming. However, more likely he disliked David's choosing Amasa to lead the army in his stead. After he killed him, one of Joab's men stood near Amasa's body and said Joab and David's supporters should follow Joab. That statement made Joab seem like he was still the king's man while alluding to Amasa's defection to Absalom. When everyone who encountered Amasa's body stopped and wouldn't proceed, someone moved him into a field and covered him (see 2 Sam. 20:8–13; 1 Kings 2:5).

Beware: *Of those resentful of your promotion but who draw close with signs of friendship.*

DAVID'S DEATH

When David became old and ill, Joab again opposed his wishes by backing Adonijah instead of Solomon for king. Perhaps Joab hadn't supported him because Solomon was young, around nineteen or twenty,[1] or because prophecies said he'd be a "man of rest" (1 Chron. 22:9). That description wouldn't fit with Joab's skills and pride as an army leader. Though David was in a weakened condition, he remembered Joab's crimes and knew about his latest affront against David's wishes. He gave his son instructions about seeking reprisal against Joab. He had several motives for wanting Solomon to dispense justice on him. He'd killed two threats to his being the army's commander—Abner (also as vengeance for his brother) and Amasa (see 2 Sam. 3:30; 19:13). He'd caused pain to David by slyly facilitating Absalom's return then later killing him. He'd killed during peacetime and "put the blood of war on his belt" (1 Kings 2:5). Joab would probably create trouble for Solomon's reign, so he said not to let Joab die in peace as an old man (see 1 Kings 2:1, 5–6, 33–34).

When Joab heard Solomon planned to kill him, he didn't stand in the dignity and courage his status implied. Instead, he fled to the tabernacle and took hold of the altar's horns. This was a sign of weakness and lack of integrity. He'd killed many in his role as David's captain of the army, and they'd gone honorably to their deaths. Now as he faced his own, he was cowardly. Solomon sent Benaiah to "strike him down" (1 Kings 2:29) because murderers couldn't claim sanctuary. When Benaiah asked him to come out, Joab refused and said he'd die there. Solomon was told about his words and said to kill him at the altar to remove any curse from him or David. That would avenge the men Joab had killed, men who were better than he. Benaiah killed Joab, who was then buried at his house (see 1 Kings 2:28–34). Ironically, this was the same place, the stone of Gibeon, where he'd killed Amasa.[2] Joab had been a great man, but he died a dishonorable death. As God's generals, we should never lose sight of our purpose, calling, and integrity if we want to finish our journey well.

Beware: *Of those who have done evil but call on God and others' mercy when facing consequences.*

CONCLUSION

David experienced many acts from those he loved—devotion, obedience, betrayal. He once said, "All who hate me whisper together against me; against me they devise my hurt.... Even my own familiar friend in whom I trusted, who ate my bread, has lifted up his heel against me" (Ps. 41:7, 9). Jesus would quote those words when he dealt with dynamics of an unfaithful friend (see John 13:18). How sad when friends become enemies, but those dynamics are an inevitable component of our destiny journeys.

DAVID'S WEAPONS: GOD'S ARSENAL

DAVID'S REFLECTIONS

Some trust in chariots, and some in horses; but we will remember the name of the LORD our God. They have bowed down and fallen; but we have risen and stand upright. (Ps. 20:7–8)

As this book has shown often, truly successful weapons are those God provides for the journey. David had access to mighty human weapons—armor, spears, Saul's and Goliath's swords, Jonathan's war gear. These effective weapons were important to warfare, but man-made weapons are limited. For the Christian, "the weapons of our warfare are not carnal" (2 Cor. 10:4), like man typically uses. During Saul's time, only he and Jonathan had swords because Israel had no blacksmiths nor technology to create iron.[1] Philistine blacksmiths made no weapons for Israel, "lest the Hebrews make swords or spears" (1 Sam. 13:19). They were dependent on the Philistines, even to sharpen their tools for a price. By human standards Philistines had a great advantage (see 1 Sam. 13:20–22). They didn't prevail over Israel, however, because the Hebrews' greatest weapons originated from the Father.

NOT TYPICAL WEAPONS

Hebrews worshipped a *now* God—"I AM WHO I AM" (Exod. 3:14). He wasn't the God of I WAS, but the God of I AM, who understood what they needed to take into each battle. He manifested when they needed Him—their Provider, Healer, The Lord Is There (see Gen. 22:14; Exod. 15:26; Ezek. 48:35). God's weapons were superior to man's flawed arsenals. In an unwinnable battle, God told Jehoshaphat the battle wasn't his, but it belonged the Lord (see 2 Chron. 20:15). Knowing that, our thinking should change. If we "labour therefore to enter into that rest" (Heb. 4:11 KJV), we realize the battle's outcome in advance. We can enter each skirmish in peace rather than fear. Try as hard as we can with the most formidable human weapons, the battle isn't won by our sufficiency (see 2 Cor. 3:5). A powerful heavenly arsenal could include many things: fasting, travail, Holy Spirit's gifts, waiting on the Lord, prophetic actions, and many more. Several times for me, the Lord has used Facebook as a tool for others' healings. People have told me that after I shared a word of knowledge, they were healed as they read my post. When He gives a battle plan, we're responsible for our obedience, but He's responsible for results. In everything, through Him we can exceed expectations (see Rom. 8:37).

Many biblical battles were won with unusual weapons. Joshua's victories occurred with hailstones, the sun's immobility, shouts after circling a wall, his leader's upraised hands (see Josh. 10:11, 13; 6:20; Exod. 17:11). Elisha's weapons were a barrage of angels or lepers' footsteps outside a camp (see 2 Kings 6:17; 7:3, 7). When the children in the wilderness were frightened and complaining, Moses told them to "stand still, and see the salvation of the Lord" (Exod. 14:13). The psalmist acknowledged this weapon's power when he said to "Be still, and know that I am God" (Ps. 46:10). What a weapon—standing still! Sometimes our role in God's plan requires actively pursuing the enemy, but now and then His weapon is silence or inactivity while He sets up victory.

On the other hand, the weapon could be just the opposite—speaking God's words. Once, a personable candidate for pastor at the church I attended didn't ring true in others' spirits, including mine. The congregation was voting the next day, and my spirit was grieved. As I prayed the night before, the Lord gave me a single, doctrinal question to ask. The next morning as we readied to vote, he surveyed us from his platform seat, his smirk saying he was assured of the outcome. Before we voted, however, I raised my hand and asked him what God had told me. His smile was immediately replaced by a glare and rant declaring that was none of my business. With a simple question authored by God, the man demonstrated his true colors, and people knew he wasn't right to shepherd their flock. God's weapons are always right.

The Lord battled often for the Hebrews. He sent a wind to push back the Red Sea, removed wheels from Egyptian chariots, then released walls of water to drown them (see Exod. 14:21, 25, 28). One of my favorite weapons is after the people left Egypt. God sent Moses on a longer journey around the Philistines' land, "Lest perhaps the people change their minds when they see war, and return to Egypt" (Exod. 13:17). That detail says volumes about the Father's love. Though often we're strong and can fight intense battles, other times we may become disheartened by extreme warfare. God knew the Hebrews hadn't experienced war during their generation, and He wouldn't allow a more difficult situation than they could handle (see 1 Cor. 10:13). Sometimes His unusual weapon is to change travel plans and take us a longer way to avoid our feeling hopeless and accepting defeat. What an amazing lesson to learn on our destiny journeys!

Many times warfare takes us into the enemy's lair; but often, God wants us to avoid the enemy because fellowshipping with evil could corrupt (see 1 Cor. 15:33). Avoidance is an amazing weapon. Those who cause divisiveness or offenses, or those who don't believe correct doctrines shouldn't be welcome in our houses (see Rom. 16:17; 2 John 10). We're "not to keep company... [with the]...sexually immoral...covetous...idolater...reviler... drunkard...extortioner—not even to eat with such a person" (1 Cor. 5:11). However, though we shouldn't affiliate with those used by satan, we can't "count [them] as an enemy, but admonish [them] as a brother" (2 Thess. 3:15). Because destiny journeys prepare us for godly purpose, if we forget to love the unlovable, God can't take us where He wants us to go. Destiny is affected by how we treat enemies *and* brothers. How wonderful He understands what will defeat enemies while protecting us!

Beware: *Of those whose companionship could negatively affect destiny.*

DAVID'S UNUSUAL WEAPONS

In David's story God provided him and others many weapons from His atypical arsenal. Some were inferior by the world's standards; but though his army's numbers may have been fewer, David knew "the chariots of God are twenty thousand, even thousands of thousands" (Ps. 68:17). Before David's birth, God's thunderous voice was the weapon Samuel's army used to conquer. Another time, an earthquake accomplished victory for Saul (see 1 Sam. 7:10; 14:15). When Saul pursued David, God used the tool of prophecy by Saul and his messengers to derail their murderous mission.

Another time, God's weapon was to hide David from the king (see 1 Sam. 19:20–21, 23.14). At Ziklag, Benjamites became part of David's mighty men. They were "armed with bows, using both the right hand and the left in hurling stones and shooting arrows with the bow" (1 Chron. 12:2). God used ambidexterity for proficiency in battle! Gadites also joined David's mighty men in the wilderness, probably at Adullam.[2] They were battle-trained, adept with weapons, fierce, fast, and courageous enough to cross the Jordan during flood time (see 1 Chron. 12:8–15). Confidence comes with His proven, unique weapons.

David had success with other great heavenly weapons I've discussed in this book— knowledge of Holy Spirit; trust in and sensitivity to God's voice; or his integrity, for example. The psalmist recognized that God,

> Shall cover you with His feathers, and under His wings you shall take refuge; His truth shall be your shield and buckler. You shall not be afraid of the terror by night, nor of the arrow that flies by day, nor of the pestilence that walks in darkness, nor of the destruction that lays waste at noonday. A thousand may fall at your side, and ten thousand at your right hand; but it shall not come near you. (Ps. 91:4–7)

OUR HANDS AND FINGERS

David said, "Blessed be the LORD my Rock, who trains my hands for war, and my fingers for battle" (Ps. 144:1). The Lord guides our hands and fingers to be skilled in warfare and powerful in battle as we anoint with oil and then lay hands on others to war against the enemy of sickness. Samuel used his hands and fingers to anoint David for destiny. David often waved his hands in worship to his Father. Those hands weren't smooth or elegant, but rough from the work he did while attending his flock. Those hands firmly grasped beards of vicious bears and lions. They learned servanthood by soothing the tortured king or taking supplies to his brothers at the front. They became strong enough to twirl a sling swiftly about his head then clutch a huge sword to cut off the giant's head. They strung the bow

Jonathan had given him. David understood that his skill in battle was because of God, who "teaches [our] hands to make war" (2 Sam. 22:35). Those hands were trained by each experience, so eventually they could adeptly hold the nation's weight.

David's fingers warred as they strummed the lyre to worship on the hillsides then to battle demonic spirits that controlled the king of God's nation. They warred as they meticulously picked up five stones to carry into the crucial battle to determine Israel's fate. Then, his fingers held that sling and placed into it one tiny missile that overcame the giant whom Israel's greatest warriors feared. God understands that each person's fingers and hands are different as he or she goes to battle. He enables our hands and fingers to be ready for each ensuing battle that step-by-step determines destiny. Whether as shepherd or ruler, David's confidence didn't come from elaborate weapons prepared for a king or the finest and largest available. His knowledge of his arsenal brought victory because those hands and fingers were tested and prepared.

CONCLUSION

David explained his attitude about weapons in his lament about Jonathan and Saul's deaths: "How the mighty have fallen, and the weapons of war perished!" (2 Sam. 1:27). Man's weapons will rust, break, be lost or stolen, grow obsolete, wear out, develop glitches. God's weapons are mighty, will never pass away, and assure a successful destiny journey. For David, God was his weapon of deliverance from enemies: His "rock...fortress...deliverer... strength...shield...horn of [his] salvation...stronghold" (Ps. 18:2).

QUESTIONS TO PONDER
(Answers in Appendix)
JOAB

1. How did Joab become leader of David's army?

2. How did the incident with Uriah demonstrate Joab's character?

3. What mistakes did Joab make with Absalom?

4. Give two examples of when Joab killed to protect his position.

5. Besides these murders, what made David tell Solomon to kill Joab after he died?

GOD'S ARSENAL

6. Describe some of God's atypical weapons.

7. What were David's and his men's unusual weapons?

8. How might God use our hands and fingers to war?

Something to Consider: How do David's friends-turned-enemies/weapons in this chapter speak about our own?

Chapter Ten

MISCELLANEOUS FRIENDS, TURNED ENEMIES

DAVID'S REFLECTIONS

For the mouth of the wicked and the mouth of the deceitful have opened against me; they have spoken against me with a lying tongue. They have also surrounded me with words of hatred, and fought against me without a cause. In return for my love they are my accusers, but I give myself to prayer. Thus they have rewarded me evil for good, and hatred for my love. (Ps. 109:2–5)

ABNER

Though friends are crucial weapons of warfare, when those friends betray trust, they also cause much grief. Abner should probably be called David's friend/enemy/friend. He represents impressive enemies, men of integrity to be respected. He was the son of Ner, Saul's uncle, so he and Saul were first cousins. David respected Abner as a man and general. As Saul's army commander, Abner was wise and adept. After victory over the giant, he brought David to the king with Goliath's head in his hand (see 1 Sam. 14:50; 17:57). However, later as Saul's general, he was probably hunting David right along with Saul. When David had sneaked into their camp, he scolded Abner for not guarding Saul, saying, "Are you not a man? And who is like you in Israel?" (see 1 Sam. 26:15–16). Saying that no warrior compared to Abner was an enormous compliment coming from God's choice for king. They were enemies, who respected one another.

ASAHEL'S DEATH

One story changed Abner's destiny's fulfillment. Judah and Israel were at war. Zeruiah, David's sister, had three sons at the battle: Abishai, Joab, and Asahel. Abner suggested to Joab that their young men fight by grasping their opponent's head and thrusting a spear into him. A fierce battle ensued, and Judah defeated Israel badly—they lost 360 men while Judah lost only nineteen. This skirmish would lead to a lengthy civil war. During this battle, Asahel kept pursuing Abner, probably to discover an opportunity to kill him. Their skills were mismatched, and Abner became irritated when the young man continued to follow. Doesn't this sound like a spiritual pre-teen who trails closely behind, hoping to interact with, gain favor, or defeat more seasoned Christians? Abner understood his immaturity, so he didn't kill him for being annoying. Although they represented different sides, he gave Asahel advice on winning the battle with the young men. He also warned Asahel to stop shadowing him because he didn't want to kill him and then face Joab (see 2 Sam. 2:12-22, 31–32). This exchange shows Abner's integrity and Joab's reputation for retribution. Abner respected Joab, his counterpart in David's army, and gave the young man a chance to cease. Sometimes warfare requires us to defer to those in higher positions or with more experience, even those whom we consider enemies.

Beware: *Of those who refuse to change despite warnings.*

Abner shows that sometimes we should warn others of what can happen if they persist in their ways. Asahel didn't heed Abner, so Abner stabbed him in the stomach so hard that the spear protruded from his back. Though

Abner was justified in war time, killing Asahel would prove bad for him. After Abner killed Joab's brother, Joab's quest for vengeance would be part of both his and Abner's destinies. To retaliate for their brother's death, Joab and Abishai pursued relentlessly. The tribe of Benjamin gathered behind Abner's group and formed a united front on top of a hill. Abner called to Joab, "Shall the sword devour forever?" (2 Sam. 2:26) and reminded him they were brothers. These words made Joab stop temporarily, but he didn't forget Abner's actions (see 2 Sam. 2:23–28).

Beware: *Of delayed actions from those whose minds are consumed with revenge.*

THE KINGDOM

After Saul's death, Abner made Saul's son, Ishbosheth, Israel's king. This was also a mistake. Saul had known prophecies about David being king; Abner had surely heard them, too. He later reiterated to Ishbosheth about David being God's chosen. Despite recognizing David's anointing, nothing indicates that Abner asked God about Ishbosheth reigning, and he certainly knew of his weaknesses. Even when tradition dictates who should rule next, if a person knows God's will and does his or her own, that's rebellion, which affects destiny. Ishbosheth reigned two years over everything but Judah. During that time, Israel and Judah were enemies, and civil war continued. Although Judah was one tribe against eleven others, God's choice for king was their leader. David grew stronger while Saul's house grew weaker (see 2 Sam. 2:8–11; 3:1).

BEWARE: *Of those who know God's will but ignore it.*

As war escalated, Abner got a stronger hold on Saul's house. Ishbosheth accused him of being with Saul's concubine, Rizpah. If this were true, being with Rizpah could give Abner claim to Saul's throne. Abner got angry at the accusation and said he'd been faithful to Saul by establishing Ishbosheth as king when he could've delivered Israel to David. Ishbosheth didn't answer because he feared Abner. However, his accusations may have finished swaying Abner toward David. His changing allegiances may also have been prompted by knowing the kingdom was failing under Ishbosheth. Abner sent David a message, saying if they made covenant, he'd bring Israel's support as king.

David agreed but only if Abner brought him Michal, David's wife and Saul's daughter, who'd been given to another (see 2 Sam. 3:6–13).

David sent messengers to Ishbosheth also asking for Michal. He reminded Ishbosheth of the dowry he'd paid for her with Philistine foreskins. Ishbosheth honored David's request and took her from her current husband, Paltiel, who followed weeping until Abner commanded him to return home. Nothing was said about David's reunion with Michal until her disdain of him when they retrieved the ark. By reclaiming Michal, David recovered his wife and asserted a claim on Saul's house since she was his daughter. Abner did as he'd promised and spoke for David to Israel's elders, even Saul's tribe, Benjamin. He reminded them how the Lord had declared that by David's hand He'd save Israel from their enemies. He traveled to Hebron to confer with David, who prepared a feast for Abner and his twenty men. He committed to gathering Israel and then made covenant with David to rule (see 2 Sam. 3:14–21; 6:16). David later sent Abner away, and he "had gone in peace" (2 Sam. 3:22), meaning their differences had been settled.[1] David's enemy had become his friend. His actions showed strength as a negotiator, a trait that would serve him well as Israel's future king.

ABNER'S DEATH

As Abner departed, Joab and David's servants returned with massive spoils from a raid. When Joab heard David had met with Abner, he confronted the king and said Abner approached to deceive and discern his army's movements. Without David's knowledge, he sent messengers to bring Abner back. After his return, Joab stopped Abner at the gate. This was wise and sly. Killing Abner inside the city would've been a great violation of the law since Hebron was a sanctuary city. Joab appeared to want a private conversation with Abner. He drew close, then stabbed him. Although Joab murdered Abner for killing his brother, he likely also slaughtered him for encroaching on his territory and threatening his leadership. Joab later killed Amasa with the same ploy of friendship and likely motive of retaining his position (see Josh. 20:6–7; 2 Sam. 3:24–27; 20:10).

Beware: *Of those who stop at nothing to preserve power and status.*

When David learned of Abner's death, he mourned and said consequences for the murder would fall on the head of Joab and his family. He respected and grieved for Abner and told Joab and everyone else to mourn, too. Though Joab must've been insincere, they all grieved. David followed the coffin, wept at the grave, and vowed to eat nothing until sunset. This pleased the people, who then understood David didn't condone Abner's death. Having others recognize his heart was important because they'd know he hadn't broken covenant with Abner. It also made greater acceptance of David as king of all Israel. Abner's death brought chaos into Israel because of Ishbosheth's weakness and reliance on Abner. Abner's murder was so significant to David that as he was dying, he left instructions for Joab to be killed, partly because of the murder (see 2 Sam. 3:28–4:1; 1 Kings 2:5).

Beware: *Of consequences for hurting a righteous person.*

AHITHOPHEL

Ahithophel, a mighty man of God, represents those who can hear from the Lord and operate in God-given gifts but allow emotions and unforgiveness to cause them to lose their way. His son was Eliam, one of David's elite mighty men and Bathsheba's dad. Uriah, her husband, was also one of the mighty men (see 1 Chron. 11:41; 2 Sam. 11:3; 23:34). In David's service as a counselor and friend, he's first mentioned during Absalom's rebellion after the scandal with Bathsheba and David. When Absalom formed his coalition against David, Ahithophel joined. David realized God talked to him and therefore Ahithophel had power and accuracy in his guidance. After he heard his counselor had changed sides, his son's defection became even harder. His friend's advice to David and now to Absalom was like he'd heard straight from the Lord (see 2 Sam. 15:12; 16:23). Because of this, David prayed that God would "turn the counsel of Ahithophel into foolishness" (2 Sam. 15:31). The meaning of Ahithophel, "brother of ruin or folly,"[2] probably evolved after David's prayer.

As Bathsheba's grandfather, Ahithophel's resentment likely stemmed from David's moral failure with her. Because Ahithophel was one of the first Absalom sent for after his coup, Absalom and Ahithophel had likely commiserated about David's lack of consequences for his sin and plotted together in the past. Although God had forgiven David, others didn't. By Hebrew law, what David had done was punishable by death for both him and Bathsheba.[3] As a man of God, perhaps knowing that David wasn't going to be killed for his sin made Ahithophel desert him. David probably thought about his trusted counsellor when he wrote as he fled from Absalom, "Lord, how they have increased who trouble me! Many are they who rise up against me… [and] …say of me, 'there is no help for him in God'" (Ps. 3:1–2).

BEWARE: *Of one who nurtures unforgiveness.*

HUSHAI

As David ascended the mountain to worship, another counselor, Hushai, approached dressed in mourning attire—a torn robe and dust on his head. Hushai later was described as the "king's companion" (1 Chron. 27:33), which meant, "king's friend."[4] He supported David against Absalom, but David told him if he aligned with them he'd be a burden. He needed Hushai for a greater purpose. If he returned to Jerusalem, he could help David's cause by being positioned to serve as David's inside man and spy to pass intel to David through priests (see 2 Sam. 15:32–36). Then, he could "defeat the counsel of Ahithophel" (2 Sam. 15:34). David's request implies he understood the strength of good counsel for leaders and knew personally about Ahithophel's wisdom.

Everyone needs good advice from others as he or she travels in each phase of his or her destiny journey. God positions people in many roles in His kingdom, and those anointed as aides to leadership have an important station. Years later when another king, Ahab, martyred God's prophets, the Lord placed a believer as an assistant in his camp—Obadiah. When Ahab and Jezebel were planning attacks against the prophets, Obadiah heard their strategies and took steps to protect God's warriors. As a result, he saved 100 prophets' lives by hiding and feeding them (see 1 Kings 18:3–4). Often we want to be anointed to serve the Lord by ruling in His kingdom in a visible leadership role. More often, though, we have an Obadiah or Hushai anointing to help the Lord's cause in a less obvious role. Every job is important, and each assignment better prepares us for God's ultimate purpose.

Beware: *Of thinking your God-appointed job is insignificant.*

WITH ABSALOM

Hushai went to Jerusalem to meet with Absalom, who questioned why he didn't follow his friend David. Hushai responded that he'd support whomever the Lord and the people chose, implying that selection was Absalom. He planned to serve David's son like he'd attended David. This appealed to Absalom's enormous ego. He accepted Hushai's explanation then asked Ahithophel's advice about attacking David. Ahithophel told Absalom to have relations with David's concubines who remained to watch the house. That act would be a great insult to David and signify that Absalom was publicly asserting claim to the throne. The nation would hear and know David hated Absalom. As a result, they'd strongly support Absalom (see 2 Sam. 16:15–21).

Perhaps Ahithophel suggested this act because he wanted David to experience the shame he and others in Bathsheba's family had endured after David slept with Uriah's wife. Whatever the reason, Ahithophel's advice was inexcusable. This was a man who heard directly from God, yet his suggestions were opposite of God's law. Often as unforgiveness festers, our walk with the Lord wanes. However, this ungodly advice appealed to Absalom. He placed his tent on David's roof and went in to the concubines to demonstrate contempt for his father (see 2 Samuel 16:22). Paul said a sexual immorality exists that can't be voiced—"a man has his father's wife" (1 Cor. 5:1). Absalom's actions remind me of Tamar's comment about committing an act that isn't spoken in Israel. Absalom committed an atrocity as horrific in God's eyes as that for which he'd killed Amnon.

Beware: *Of those who use God's gifts to get even with another.*

DUELING COUNSELLORS

Ahithophel made a second proposal that night. Because this was the night of the same day David had fled from Jerusalem,[5] his group was probably weary and disorganized. Ahithophel asked to choose 12,000 men he'd lead to pursue David (see 2 Sam. 17:1). A surprise attack would catch David, "weary and weak, and make him afraid. And all the people who [were] with him [would] flee" (2 Sam. 17:2). This was strong counsel but presumptive. Ahithophel was a counselor, not a man of war. His wanting to lead the large group into battle showed his anger and need for retribution. His plan also presumed David's men had such little loyalty that they'd desert him; and if David were killed, others would follow Absalom in peace. This plan had merit, but Ahithophel may have been tainted by his feelings of unforgiveness and betrayal. His choosing to desert David could've clouded his perception of how others would react to the king.

This advice pleased Absalom and his elders, but he called Hushai for a second opinion. After he reiterated Ahithophel's plan, Hushai then did what David had prayed—he defeated Ahithophel's sound insight. He advised Absalom that Ahithophel's good recommendation wouldn't work at that time. David and his mighty men were currently riled up like a mama bear whose cubs have been taken. Hushai said because David was a man of war, he wouldn't camp but was probably already hidden somewhere to ambush them. If Absalom sustained a defeat, people would lose heart. Then, loyalties would revert to David because they knew him and his army as mighty men (see 2 Sam. 17:4–10).

Hushai suggested Absalom gather Israel around him and war in person against David. They would find him, pounce, and annihilate him and his men. If David were hiding in a city, they'd leave not even a stone and pull that city into the river with ropes. Absalom and the people agreed that Hushai's advice was better than Ahithophel's. God had David's back and subverted Ahithophel's good advice to "bring disaster on Absalom" (2 Sam. 17:14). Although David could do nothing to stop Absalom's takeover, God could, by changing others' perceptions of Ahithophel's advice (see 2 Sam. 17:11–14).

After Hushai passed along the warning, David's men hid in a well, and Absalom's group unsuccessfully sought to capture them. After Absalom's men left, David's spies emerged from the well and hurried to him. They told him to cross over the water because Ahithophel had given accurate counsel against the king. David and his people traversed the Jordan, so no one was left by morning (see 2 Sam. 17:15, 18, 21–22). When Ahithophel realized Absalom hadn't followed his advice, he should've felt that once again he'd provided sound counsel. He could've acknowledged his mistake in backing Absalom, who was disloyal and immature in seeking then acting on Hushai's advice. He could've thought Absalom unworthy of the gifts he had to offer and returned to David, who surely would've welcomed back his friend, his confidant, his wife's grandfather. Instead, he saddled his donkey, went home to the city, "put his household in order, and hanged himself, and died" (2 Sam. 17:23). How heartbreaking that a man described as hearing directly from God would respond this way to rejection! His amazing destiny journey ended tragically because he held onto hurt.

Beware: *Of your response when people don't act on your advice or prophetic words.*

SHEBA

Another of Saul's descendants wreaked havoc for David. Sheba represents opportunists with self-serving motives who take advantage of another's troubles to stir up antagonism against leadership. These are common enemies who have destiny potential, but their attitudes preclude them from succeeding. They believe they can do *your* ministry better than *you* can. They criticize leadership's choices, go on the offensive when anyone confronts them, and make life difficult for leaders. Sheba first appeared when David was restored to the throne after Absalom died. As a Benjamite, Sheba was probably upset that Judah, not Benjamin, ruled. He rebelled by blowing a trumpet to declare they had no share or inheritance in David then ordering every man of Israel to go to his tent. Although previously Israel had boasted they were first to welcome David back after Absalom's rebellion, now they were first to ally with Sheba. Every man of Israel deserted David to follow this usurper, but Judah's men stayed loyal. In Jerusalem, David secluded his concubines he'd left to keep the house and ensured their safety.

His caring for them before battle was an act of kindness. From then on, though, he supported them but didn't go in to them (see 2 Sam. 20:1–3), probably because they'd been with Absalom. After David assembled his men to fight, the incident with Joab and Amasa ensued.

Beware: *Of those who take advantage of leadership's struggles to make a power play.*

David told Abishai of the necessity for swiftness because Sheba's rebellion would do more harm than Absalom had. Perhaps that was because of the feud between Judah and Benjamin or because Israel was beginning to heal after Absalom's insurrection and exorbitant loss of his countrymen's lives. After Amasa's death, Joab gathered men, besieged Sheba at Beth Maachah, built a mound, and battered the wall. A wise woman cried out from the city and asked to speak to Joab. She said she was one of the peaceful and faithful who recalled disputes being settled by talking rather than by God's people destroying one another. Joab said destruction wasn't his intent; if they delivered Sheba, his army would leave. The woman promised that Sheba's head would come over the wall. She assembled others in the city; together they cut off his head and threw it over. Joab blew the trumpet and everyone withdrew to his tent. People returned to Jerusalem, and Joab was again the leader of David's army (see 2 Sam. 20:6, 15–23). Sheba's destiny wasn't to commandeer David's; but whatever his destiny was to be, he couldn't fulfill it because of misguided dreams of grandeur.

Beware: *Of those who attack rather than talk.*

ADONIJAH

David once again faced opposition from a son, this time as Adonijah opposed his father's choice of successor. He represents those whose destinies can't happen because they aren't submissive. They feel entitled to kingdom positions rather than accepting God's selections. He nearly derailed Solomon's destiny, but David's friends intervened. Adonijah, means "the Lord is my master,"[6] but his name belies his actions. He knew God's preference and defied it. Apparently, Chileab, David's second son, had died young because Adonijah was now the oldest. The fourth son of David, he was born to Haggith (see 2 Sam. 3:4). Although they had different mothers, Adonijah probably looked up to and emulated the deceptive ways of his older brother, Absalom. Being next in line, he seemed like a good choice to lead, but he should've known by his father's history that good choices aren't necessarily God's choices.

David had failed in rearing most of his kids; lack of discipline had produced prideful, rebellious, sinful, murderous children. Like Absalom, Adonijah was good-looking, spoiled, entitled, and rebellious because David "had not rebuked him at any time by saying, 'Why have you done so?'" (1 Kings 1:6). David should've known the importance of discipline in training his sons to be leaders of integrity. Eli and Samuel had been godly priests who'd reared terrible children (see 1 Sam. 3:13; 8:3). Leaders, especially, should correct their children so they grow up to be righteous, respectful men and women of integrity who can step into their purposes.

Beware: *Of your desire to placate rather than discipline those for whom you have charge.*

BUILDING HIS FOLLOWERS

Much opposition against our destiny assignment is from those who attack by undermining. Years before as David had prepared for building God's house, he'd assembled Israel's elders. He spoke about erecting the temple in the future and said Solomon would rule and construct it. Adonijah had surely heard David's proclamation and later said he knew Solomon was God's choice (see 1 Chron. 28:5–6; 1 Kings 2:15). However, like when Saul stalked David to destroy him though God's anointing was apparent, Adonijah pursued his kingship, despite what God or his father wanted. He said, "*I will be king*" (1 Kings 1:5). Anytime *our* will supersedes *God's*, we're doomed to fail. As David was dying, Adonijah exploited his weakened condition like Absalom had taken advantage of his countrymen's negative feelings toward his dad. Also like Absalom, Adonijah surreptitiously garnered support then proclaimed himself king. He prepared chariots, horsemen, and fifty men to run before him. He must've had great persuasive powers because he enticed some of David's most loyal supporters to confirm allegiance: Joab (David's captain) and Abiathar (David's priest) both followed him. Other priests and David's mighty men didn't (see 1 Kings 1:5, 7–8). Destiny isn't fulfilled if we scheme to make it happen despite what God wants.

Beware: *Of those who care more about their ambitions than leadership's and God's choices.*

NATHAN'S PLAN

Nathan, who knew God had chosen Solomon, told Bathsheba about Adonijah declaring his kingship and that David didn't know. He advised her about how to save Solomon's heritage and hers and Solomon's lives. She should approach David and ask if he'd promised that Solomon would succeed him. If so, why had Adonijah become king? After she said this to David, Nathan would arrive and confirm her words. When she entered his chamber and gave homage, David asked what she wanted. She told him Nathan's words about the sacrifice and that Solomon wasn't invited. Israel was looking to David to know his successor; therefore, he needed to inform the nation. If he didn't, after he died, she and Solomon would be considered offensive and be killed (see 1 Kings 1:11–21).

As Bathsheba talked to David, Nathan appeared and repeated her concerns. He told him about the sacrifice and that Adonijah had invited his brothers and Judah's men. However, many of David's supporters were blatantly missing: Nathan, Zadok, Benaiah, or Solomon. Those attending were chanting support for Adonijah. David vowed again that Solomon would be king. Swiftly and authoritatively, he called for Zadok; Nathan; and Benaiah, whom he told to take servants and let Solomon ride David's mule to Gihon. Jewish tradition said riding the king's mule without permission was a capital offense, so people would know David had sanctioned Solomon as king.[7] At Gihon, Zadok and Nathan would anoint Solomon then blow the horn and say, "Long live King Solomon!" (1 Kings 1:34). He should sit on David's throne as ruler of Israel and Judah to represent his being king in David's place. Benaiah should pronounce a blessing that God would be with Solomon greater than He was with David. These men did what

David delineated. After Zadok took the horn of oil from the tabernacle and anointed Solomon, they blew the horn and shouted accolades. People rejoiced so loudly "the earth seemed to split with their sound" (1 Kings 1:40) as they followed after them, playing flutes (see 1 Kings 1:22–27, 30, 32–40).

Beware: *Of those who support leadership chosen with self-serving criteria.*

ADONIJAH'S REACTION

Adonijah was hosting a great party for his followers. Everyone was likely excited about his own potential role in Adonijah's kingdom after the coup's success. They were probably laughing and talking loudly about plans for King Adonijah's nation. They didn't seem to remember what happened to David's last son who wanted to be king despite God's choice. In just a second, God can make enemy strategies fall apart. As they were finishing, Adonijah and his guests heard that earth-shattering sound from Solomon's camp. As Joab inquired about it, Abiathar's son, Jonathan, entered. Adonijah praised his character then asked for good news. However, moods changed when Jonathan recounted what had happened, who was involved, and how Solomon was on the throne with David's blessing. He said, "They have gone up from there rejoicing, so that the city is in an uproar" (1 Kings 1:45). He added that David's servants had expressed their desire for Solomon to be greater than David, and the king was glad he'd lived to see Solomon sit on his throne. Hearing this, guests grew frightened and scattered (see 1 Kings 1:41–49).

Fearing Solomon, Adonijah took hold of the altar's horns as a sign of sanctuary. Someone told Solomon that his brother had sought sanctuary and asked Solomon not to put him to death. Unlike when Joab later did this, Solomon granted Adonijah's plea for leniency. The difference between the two offenders was that Adonijah hadn't murdered anyone. Joab had unjustly killed two people, plus Absalom. Solomon's forgiving Adonijah was unusual. During those days, not only were "pretenders" executed, but an incoming king put his brothers to death because of their potential as usurpers of the throne.[8] Solomon agreed to let him live if Adonijah proved himself worthy. If he were wicked, he'd die. Solomon asked them to bring him from the altar. Adonijah fell before the new king, who sent Adonijah to his house (see 1 Kings 1:50–53). This decision was wisdom on Solomon's part. Adonijah was his brother, and his mercy showed a great contrast between the two. During this destiny journey, we can't forget mercy, even to enemies.

Beware: *Of those who've tasted power they don't want to relinquish.*

AFTER DAVID'S DEATH

After David died, Adonijah tried more subtly to seize the kingdom. He approached Bathsheba, supposedly in peace. This common enemy tactic is employed to defeat us through one we love, the weakest link in our defense. Because he was a consummate manipulator, Adonijah probably told her how lovely she looked and praised her son's proficiency in ruling. Her initial suspicion likely eased with his kindness and ploys of flattery; after all, this was her son's brother. When he was sure she didn't perceive him as hostile, he eased into his devious purpose. Although Israel had expected the kingdom to be his, the Lord turned it over to Solomon. He then again revealed his untrustworthy nature. He asked her to petition Solomon for Abishag to be his wife. When David had been old; ill; and very cold, probably feverish, covers couldn't take away his chills. They'd appointed Abishag, a young Shunammite virgin, to care for his needs, lie with, and warm him. She was David's companion during his last days. Adonijah wanted her now (see 1 Kings 2:13–17; 1:1–4).

Beware: *Of those with dubious histories who draw near in friendship.*

When Bathsheba approached to appeal to Solomon, he obviously had great respect and affection for his mother. He'd made a seat for her by his right hand, a position of power. He rose and bowed as she entered. When she said she had a small request, Solomon responded that he wouldn't refuse. However, when she asked for Abishag be given to Adonijah, he reacted angrily. Although he hadn't yet been granted supernatural wisdom that later defined him, he already showed understanding of the enemy. He would write, "Wisdom is the principal thing" and "better than weapons of war" (Prov. 4:7; Eccles. 9:18). This time he acted from that philosophy. She'd been exploited to convince him to perform an act with negative consequences. That request would be similar to Absalom's going in to his dad's concubines or Ishbosheth's accusing Abner of sleeping with Rizpah. Giving Abishag to Adonijah would provide claim to the kingdom because she'd been part of David's harem. Solomon said Adonijah's speaking these words had brought about his death. Because he'd again attempted to undermine, Solomon sent Benaiah to slay Adonijah that day (see 1 Kings 2:19–25). Character matters greatly when God assigns destinies.

Beware: *Of those who try to cheat you through someone you love and respect.*

ABIATHAR

Abiathar represents a friend who's loyal to his leader but abandons allegiance to the leader's successor. He was a man of excellence and the one remaining priest at Nob after Doeg's slaughter. One of Ahimelech's sons, Abiathar, escaped and fled to David. Later references to Abiathar call him the high priest when David got showbread, so Abiathar and David were already acquainted before the Nob disaster (see 1 Sam. 22:20–23; Mark 2:26). Because David was Saul's enemy, Abiathar would be, too; so David said, "Stay with me, do not fear. For he who seeks my life seeks your life, but with me you shall be safe" (1 Sam. 22:23).

Beware: *Of those who count you as an enemy because of your associations.*

After he aligned with David, Abiathar was mentioned several times. David had gone to Keilah after Nob. After praying for direction, David defeated the Philistines, who were plundering Keilah. When he heard of Saul's plans to attack at Keilah, he asked Abiathar to bring the ephod for direction. When he and his men returned to their camp at Ziklag, the Amalekites had ravaged them. The result was to draw David closer to God. He found strength and focus when Abiathar brought the ephod to see if he should pursue. Later, after David was king, he asked God twice about going against the Philistines. Although Abiathar wasn't mentioned, he probably was part of those times, too. While David was being chased by Absalom,

Abiathar was David's loyal friend. As Zadok and the priests bore the ark to the wilderness and set it down, Abiathar stood on the mountain until everyone had crossed. Then, David told Zadok, Abiathar, Jonathan, and the Levites to take the ark back to Jerusalem. He'd return if it were God's will and asked them to send for him when it was okay. Abiathar and Zadok were also situated so Hushai could pass along battle strategies and messages to David through priests (see 1 Sam. 23:5–9; 2 Sam. 5:19, 23; 15:24–25, 35).

HIS BETRAYAL

After many years of Abiathar's loyalty to David, his actions at the end of David's life changed those dynamics. Though Abiathar had followed David during Absalom's rebellion, when Adonijah wanted to steal Solomon's promised kingship, Abiathar became part of Adonijah's supporters, despite knowing the king's and God's plans. What motivated this is unclear, but his son Jonathan was also among those following Adonijah. They obviously had deep devotion to David. When Jonathan entered the feast, he showed that loyalty to David by saying, "Our lord King David" (1 Kings 1:43), but they didn't acknowledge his choice of successors. After David died, Solomon told Abiathar he deserved death for this betrayal, but Solomon wouldn't sentence him to die because he'd carried the ark for David and suffered the same afflictions as his father. However, he removed him as a priest. This fulfilled the prophecy that Eli's house would be removed from serving as priests. Solomon then made Benaiah head of the army and Zadok (who'd run the tabernacle) the priest instead of Abiathar (see 1 Kings 1:7; 2:26–27, 35; 1 Sam. 2:31).

CONCLUSION

When those we love become enemies to derail God's plan, we'll be hurt. David said, "Fierce witnesses rise up… They reward me evil for good..... But as for me, when they were sick, my clothing was sackcloth.... But in my adversity they rejoiced and gathered together…against me, and I did not know it; they tore at me and did not cease" (Ps. 35:11–13, 15). Even though we ache as we endure betrayal, He has every aspect of our destinies in His hand. Everything will work for our promotions.

QUESTIONS TO PONDER
(Answers in Appendix)
MISCELLANEOUS FRIENDS, TURNED ENEMIES

1a. Explain this section's title.

1b. List examples.

2. How did Asahel die?

3. Why did Abner support David as king?

4. Ahithophel probably defected to Absalom because of what event?

5. Why is Adonijah in this chapter?

6. Why didn't Solomon kill Abiathar?

Something to Consider: How do David's friends-turned-enemies in this chapter speak about our friends-turned-enemies today?

MY HUSBAND'S THOUGHTS

By Wade Urban

David's life is a portrait of the anointing in believers' lives. His transformation from boy to man after God's heart reveals principles concerning the anointing for a God-chosen destiny. He received God's imputed power through Holy Spirit to do Jesus' works. Aspects of David's anointing are active for us as well:

❖ Anointing determines destiny!

David was an unlikely choice as Israel's next king. He was tending his father's flocks, yet God instructed Samuel to anoint him. David's destiny was determined by God, and Holy Spirit's power propelled him through every challenge to his calling. Neither David's failures nor successes kept him from fulfilling his destiny. Just as the anointing made him a "marked man," so will your anointing define purpose and determine destiny.

❖ Anointing attracts attacks!

David's life was marked by conflict and warfare. His anointing enraged an envious Saul who sought to murder him, yet David was protective and respectful of the current king. When the Philistines attacked, the anointing prevailed. Amalekites looted David's camp at Ziklag, yet the anointing restored everything. Soon afterwards, David was appointed king over Judah. Many question being in God's will because of a barrage of attacks. You're attacked *because* you're in His will, but your anointing is greater than all satan's power. Keep believing, confessing God's word, praising, and worshiping, and you'll triumph in Christ (see 2 Cor. 2:14).

❖ Anointing is faith-fueled!

David had faith in God's covenant promises. Faith fueled his anointing that transformed a boy on an errand into a mighty warrior who felled a giant. His life was faith-filled. Faith in God's unseen and unfulfilled promise ignited David's anointing to keep him rising to the top. Faith activates Holy Spirit's power within us, so He's able to do exceedingly abundantly above all we ask or think (see Eph. 3:20).

❖ Anointing releases revelation!

David yearned for intimacy with the Lord. When confronted by his enemies, he withdrew to his secret place where he received God's direction. He'd reveal tactics to David, who used God's wisdom for victory. His anointing as a psalmist released prophetic revelation of the Suffering Savior (see Ps. 22); Good Shepherd (see Ps. 23); and other psalms of praise and worship that have comforted, encouraged, and enlightened throughout generations. Believers' anointing today releases Holy Spirit's revelation through the gifts. Revelation isn't just for a pastor, evangelist, prophet, or teacher but for every believer!

❖ Anointing produces power!

Believers' anointing produces power to conduct spiritual warfare against the devil's wiles and tactics and pull down strongholds (see Eph. 6:10–18; 2 Cor. 10:3–6). David's anointing killed Goliath, conquered enemies, and gave supernatural power to war. The anointing produced power to be a witness of God's covenant promises. David exercised dominion over uncircumcised enemies. His life was a witness to every Israelite of God's wonder-working power. He was desperate for God's presence and went to great lengths to transport His ark to Jerusalem. True worship occurs when we come to the end of ourselves and expose our inner selves before God, not concerned with what others think. In Jerusalem he ordered Levites to conduct praise and worship services 24/7 before God's tabernacle for the duration of his reign as king. The anointing for worship requires Holy Spirit's power; true worship cannot be taught, imitated, or delegated.

❖ Anointing begets breakthrough!

When Philistines gathered against him in the Valley of Rephaim, David inquired of God, went against them, and defeated them. The battleground was named Baal Perazim, meaning "the Lord has broken through." The anointing "breaks through" satanic barriers with which satan intends to defeat us. Spiritual death, bodily disease, financial and spiritual poverty, and sin's condemnation have no power over lives if we understand our heritage in Christ. Truth makes us free (see John 8:31–32), and anointing teaches truth and begets breakthrough!

❖ Anointing transforms messes into miracles!

While in Gath, David pretended insanity, drooling onto his beard and scratching at a door. His ruse worked and allowed him to escape into the cave Adullam. It became a testimony as the anointing transformed 400 outcasts into mighty men of valor, noted for mighty deeds. The anointing transformed what a pastor would call a "mess" into a "miracle!" Jesus' earthly ministry was turning messes into miracles. As new creations in Christ (see 2 Cor. 5:17), we've been anointed to transform messes into miracles!

AFTERWORD

Through one trial, one victory, one step at a time, we move toward destiny. With each level, we encounter those who want us to fail and turn back instead of moving into what God has planned. Enemies come in all shapes and sizes, but their motivation and purpose is the same. Satan is using them to disrupt our arriving at and fulfilling destiny. My husband says that with battles, we're always in one of three positions—in a battle, just finishing one, or going into one. The enemy wants us defeated; so we can be assured he'll regularly accost us, and often in a manner we're not expecting. Despite that, we shouldn't operate in fear or with a defeated mindset. Each day as we rise, we can don our armor and do whatever God reveals for battle. Then we should rest in Him because He takes care of His warriors, whether actively fighting on the front lines or recuperating from prior wounds. David maneuvered many adversities, yet stepped into and performed his God-ordained destiny. As I said in the "Prologue," his life experiences can teach us much about our own warfare and experiences with the Lord. David's enemies and how he overcame them teaches us that God has a plan for our success.

ANSWERS TO "QUESTIONS TO PONDER"

CHAPTER ONE – SAUL AND OBEDIENCE

1. He changed from being humble to being disobedient, untruthful, self-serving, easily insulted.

2a. Saul had killed his 1,000's; David, his 10,000's.

2b. Jealousy, hatred, suspicion, fear

3. He hoped Philistines would kill David when he got the dowry for Michal. He asked Jonathan and his servants to kill him. He twice tried to kill him while David ministered to him. He sent men to David's and Michal's house to kill him.

4. David received food, direction, and a weapon from the priest. Saul heard and had his servant Doeg kill priests, women, children, and infants.

5. Saul went into a cave to use the bathroom, and David and Abishai breached Saul's camp while they slept.

6a. Philistines were going against him, and God no longer spoke to him. He wanted to consult Samuel, who was dead.

6b. Philistines defeated Israel and killed Saul and his sons.

7a. With unquestioning, immediate obedience

7b. Abraham, Mary, Philip

8a. He didn't utterly destroy everything.

8b. Pride, disobedience, lying, not accepting responsibility

9. Even if disobedience is for a good reason, obedience is more important.

10. He didn't seek God's will. He implied Israel was strong on its own.

CHAPTER TWO – ABSALOM AND TRIALS

1. Long hair, good looks

2a. He lured Tamar into his bedroom under false pretenses then raped her.

2b. He advised Tamar to be quiet then planned revenge.

3. He waited a long time until he could enact revenge. Then he had Amnon go somewhere so he could kill him.

4. He went to live with his grandfather. He made Joab ask David if he could return.

6. He created a small army then sat at the gate to hear people's cases.

7. His hair caught on a tree limb, and he was left hanging. Joab and his men stabbed him.

8. How things heat up to purify us as gold or silver

9. Misfits—in distress, debt, discontented

10. When David returned from being with Achish, Amalekites had raided their camp at Ziklag. They'd burned the camp, taken their goods, and kidnapped their families.

11. Patience, elimination of undesirable traits, etc.

12. David sent servants to pay his respect to Hanun's dad. Hanun thought they were spies, so he shaved off half their beards and cut off their clothes to their buttocks.

13. Get up!

CHAPTER THREE – THE PHILISTINES AND WORSHIP

1. Eli

2a. Broken idols, tumors, rats

2b. If we take what isn't ours, trouble will follow.

3. He pretended to be crazy.

4. Philistine princes wouldn't allow David to fight against Saul because they were Hebrews.

5. The first time David attacked. The second time he waited until he heard marching in the treetops.

6. We should consistently worship God in all we do.

7. He worshipped before battle and won an impossible victory.

8a. When we feel least like worshiping

8b. When Saul was possessed, when his baby died, after Absalom and Ahithophel deserted him, while he was dying and his son violated his wishes

9. Stones, sheep, cows, everything with or without breath

10. She criticized how David worshipped and became barren.

CHAPTER FOUR – GOLIATH AND HOLY SPIRIT

1. One person whose victory or defeat represented the entire army

2. Israelites were frightened and fled. David relied on God and volunteered to fight.

3. Weapons not used enough to be familiar with them

4. He belittled him then acted insulted that Israel would send someone so insignificant against him. He made bold claims of what he'd do to David.

5. At first they were disbelieving. Then Israel rejoiced and pursued while Philistines fled.

6. He dwelt *with* them but now dwells *in* us.

7. Infilling comes with salvation. We activate His gifts by being "filled with" Holy Spirit, with evidence of speaking in tongues.

8. Revelation—words of knowledge, words of wisdom, discernment of spirits; Speaking—prophecy, different kinds of tongues, interpretation of tongues; Power—gift of faith, gifts of healings, working of miracles

9. Belt of truth, breastplate of righteousness, gospel of peace, shield of faith, helmet of salvation, sword of the Spirit

10. Prophetic actions—circle around behind trees; prophecy—killing Goliath, with worship, about Jesus; method of operation—sling and stone; discernment of spirits—Saul's demons; unction – feeling bad after numbering people

11. He prophesied while he held a spear to kill David. His heart was full of hate, envy, fear, anger, etc.

Chapter Five – Shimei and The Anointing

1. He was from Saul's house and resented David's being king.

2. Being blood thirsty, killing Saul's family

3. He wanted to kill him.

4. It may have been God's will that he attacked David.

5. Bring his gray head to the grave with blood

6. He made him promise to stay in Jerusalem. He did for three years then left to retrieve a slave.

7. Being called is the potential to work for God. Being chosen is when we're qualified to serve in our destinies.

8. David, Moses, 2 Marys, Gideon, Amos, Disciples, Saul

9. Holy Spirit's empowerment to do His will

10. Attacks, favor, covering from poor choices

Chapter Seven – Jonathan and Relationship/His Presence

1. He and his armor bearer killed several Philistines then set up a great Israeli victory.

2a. He'd disobeyed Saul's orders about eating.

2b. He elevated his orders above God's. He didn't want to kill those who rushed on animals in violation of God's commands but ordered his son's death.

3. Defended David, refused to kill him, hid him, made covenant with him

4. Unbreakable promise with rewards for obedience and punishments for disobedience

5a. He was Jonathan's son, who was crippled while running away after his family's deaths. When David discovered he was alive, he restored his lands, brought him to the palace, and let him eat at his table.

5b. He said he'd stayed in Jerusalem because he was glad Absalom was rebelling. Saul's kingdom would be restored to him.

6. Revelation, relationship, trust in His ability

7. Having a defeated attitude

8. Moses talked to God face-to-face.

9. To be in God's presence

10. Where we're alone to communicate with God

CHAPTER EIGHT – SIGNIFICANT PROPHETS AND GOD'S WORD/TRUST

1. Both heard from God as children, learned obedience, grieved for Saul, were men of prayer, and the Lord was with them.

2. They wanted to be like other nations and seemed to rely on a king's power rather than God's.

3. It positioned him to sin with Bathsheba.

4. He looked, let his eye linger, acted on his lust, and tried to cover it up.

5. He called David out for his sin, which allowed him to repent. Later, he corrected what he said about David building God's house.

6. The Word is powerful enough to cut down enemy attacks but can also divide our private thoughts from intentions.

7. It's ultimate truth for correction, instruction, equipping.

8. Whatever we say speaks that into our lives—faith, fear, etc.

9. He let his fate be in God's hand.

10. After Abraham prayed for Abimelech, his wives' barrenness left, and Sarah conceived. Job was restored after he prayed for his friends.

CHAPTER EIGHT – MISCELLANEOUS ENEMIES AND FRIENDS AND INTEGRITY/PREPARATION

1. They attacked weaker ones.

2. They'd been physically unable to go.

3. He didn't want Israel to harm Lot's descendants.

4. His name means "foolish," and he was.

5. She brought supplies then told him that harming Nabal might affect his kingship.

6. He was faithful to David.

7. He listed some of their feats.

8. Uriah

9. David invited him to Jerusalem then asked Solomon to show kindness to Barzillai's sons and let them eat at his table.

10. Integrity and preparation

11. Actions demonstrate character.

12. With Saul, Ishbosheth, sheep, etc.

13. Saul was anointed shortly before he took office, but David had many years of preparation. Saul wasn't ready, but David was.

14. He cares for and protects the flock rather than being self-serving.

CHAPTER NINE – JOAB AND GOD'S ARSENAL

1. He was first to climb the water shaft and defeat Jebusites.

2. He complied with David's wishes and ordered Uriah to the hottest part of battle.

3. He talked David into letting him come back and then killed Absalom.

4. Amasa and Abner

5. Shedding innocent blood. Deceiving him about Absalom then killing him

6. Sun standing still, silence, marching, etc.

7. Holy Spirit, hiding, ambidexterity, integrity, etc.

8. Anoint with oil, raise in worship, hold a weapon, etc.

CHAPTER TEN – MISCELLANEOUS FRIENDS, TURNED ENEMIES

1a. Some who were David's friends ultimately became disloyal.

1b. Abner, Ahithophel, Adonijah

2. He pursued Abner, who tired of it. He killed him after warning him to stop.

3. Judah was winning the war, Ishbosheth had accused him of sleeping with Rizpah, Abner and David made covenant.

4. David's sin with Bathsheba, his granddaughter

5. He was David's son but disregarded David's wishes for Solomon to reign.

6. He'd borne the ark and suffered many things with David.

NOTES

PROLOGUE

1   "Interpreting Dictionary." The Holy Bible. Gordonsville, TN: Dugan Publishers, Inc., 1984. 3.

2   Hayford, Jack W., and D. Litt, et al. *New Spirit Filled Life Bible.* Nashville: Thomas Nelson Bibles, Thomas Nelson, Inc., 2002. "Bottom Note," 381.

3   Cook, F.C., ed. *Bible Commentary on the Old Testament.* Grand Rapids, Michigan: Baker Book House, 1981, Vol., 1 Samuel-Esther, 81.

CHAPTER ONE – SAUL

1   Cook, 46.

2   Ibid., 347.

3   Ibid., 52.

4   Ibid., 119.

DAVID'S WEAPONS: OBEDIENCE

1   Ibid., 38

CHAPTER TWO – ABSALOM

1   "Interpreting," 1.

2   *NKVJ Foundation Study Bible, The Holy Bible.* Nashville: Thomas Nelson, 2015. "Bottom Note," 344.

3   Cook, 138.

DAVID'S WEAPONS: TRIALS

1   "Interpreting," 1.
2   "How Do Oysters Make Pearls?" *HowStuffWorks*, a division of InfoSpace Holdings, LLC. (Apr. 2021): https://animals.howstuffworks.com/marine-life/question630.htm.
3   Hayford, "Bottom Note." 414.
4   Mansfield, Stephen. *Healing Your Church Hurt: What to Do When You Still Love God But Have Been Wounded by His People.* (2021): https://www.goodreads.com/author/quotes/14035.Stephen_Mansfield.

CHAPTER THREE – THE PHILISTINES

1   Foundation, "Bottom Note," 294.
2   Cook, 16.
3   Hayford, "Bottom Note," 367.
4   Cook, 17.
5   Hayford, "Bottom Note," 409.

DAVID'S WEAPONS: WORSHIP

1   *Foundation*, "Bottom Note," 356.
2   Strong, James, LL.D., S.T.D. *King James New Strong's Exhaustive Concordance.* Nashville: Thomas Nelson Publishers, 2001. G4352.
3   Ibid., G2323.
4   "Interpreting," 6.
5   Strong, H5401.
6   Howard, Jacqueline. "Cows' Moos Carry A Lot More Meaning Than You Ever Imagined," HuffPost, (Dec. 2014): https://www.huffpost.com/entry/how-cows-communicate_n_6341046.
7   Cook, 18.
8   Hayford, "Bottom Note." 409.
9   Ibid., "Bottom Note." 410.
10 Strong, G2999.
11 Ibid., H7812.

CHAPTER FOUR – GOLIATH

1   "Interpreting," 4.
2   Hayford, "Bottom Note." 381.
3   Cook, 42.

4   Hayford, "Bottom Note." 381.

5   *Foundation,* "Bottom Note." 309.

6   Cook, 42.

7   *Foundation,* 310.

8   Cook, 45.

DAVID'S WEAPONS: HOLY SPIRIT

1   Strong, G4487

2   Hayford, "Middle Note." 384.

3   Strong, H5012.

CHAPTER FIVE – SHIMEI

1   "Interpreting," 9.

2   *Foundation,* 346.

3   "Interpreting," 8.

DAVID'S WEAPONS: THE ANOINTING

1   Strong, G2822.

2   Ibid., G1588.

3   Urban, Connie Hunter. *Be Healed!,* Shippensburg, PA: Destiny Image Publishers, Inc., 2019. 110.

4   Lowell, James Russell. "The Present Crisis." Poets.org, Academy of American Poets, (No update date): https://www.poets.org/poetsorg/poem/present-crisis.

CHAPTER SEVEN – JONATHAN

1   "Interpreting," 6.

2   Strong, H5916.

3   Dake, Finis Jennings. *Dake's Annotated Reference Bible.* Lawrenceville, GA: Dake Publishing, Inc. 1999. 291.

4   Cook, 139.

DAVID'S WEAPONS: RELATIONSHIP and HIS PRESENCE

1   Strong, H3427.

2   "Interpreting," 5.

CHAPTER EIGHT – SIGNIFICANT PROPHETS

1 "Interpreting," 8.
2 Cook, 29.
3 "Interpreting," 7.
4 *Foundation*, "Bottom Note," 452.
5 Cook, 96.

DAVID'S WEAPONS: GOD'S WORD and TRUST

1 Crouch, Andrae. "Through It All." *Genius*. (2021): https://genius.com/Andrae-crouch-through-it-all-lyrics.
2 Strong, G3056.
3 Cook, 39.

CHAPTER EIGHT – MISCELLANEOUS ENEMIES and FRIENDS

1 "Interpreting," 1.
2 *Foundation*, 325.
3 "Interpreting," 1.
4 *Foundation*, 340.
5 "Interpreting," 7.
6 Cook, 58.
7 *Foundation*, 457.
8 Cook, 365.

DAVID'S WEAPONS: INTEGRITY and PREPARATION

1 Strong, H8537.
2 Ibid., H8394.
3 Ibid., H7462.
4 Cook, 354.
5 Ibid., 357.
6 *Foundation*, 464.

CHAPTER TEN – JOAB

1 Cook, 143.
2 Ibid., 146.

DAVID'S WEAPONS: GOD'S ARSENAL

1   *Foundation*, 303.
2   Cook, 340.

CHAPTER ELEVEN – MISCELLANEOUS FRIENDS, TURNED ENEMIES

1   *Foundation*, 330.
2   "Interpreting," 1.
3   Hayford, "Bottom Note." 416.
4   Cook, 364.
5   Ibid., 106.
6   "Interpreting," 1.
7   Cook, 141.
8   Ibid., 142.